Common Sense
for Humans

Common Sense for Humans

An Outsider's look from the Inside

Claus Windelev

2016

ISBN: 153469899X
ISBN 13: 9781534698994

Dedicated to my granddaughter

Sofia River

Who will hopefully benefit from the power of Common Sense

List of Contents

Introduction to "Common Sense for Humans"

"COMMON SENSE": INFLUENTIAL revolutionary pamphlet by Thomas Paine, published in Philadelphia, January 1776. Paine stressed the logic of America's independence, emphasizing the defects of Britain's monarchy and the economic costs of participating in Britain's repeated European wars. Reconciliation with Britain, Paine wrote, would constitute "madness and folly." "Common Sense" avoided abstract philosophy, favoring instead the ordinary language of artisans and biblical examples to support Paine's arguments. The "plain truth" (Paine's original title for the tract) he espoused found a broad readership; around one hundred thousand copies circulated in 1776 alone, and the pamphlet stirred politicians and ordinary citizens to embrace American independence.

Bibliography: *U.S. Encyclopedia*
Conway, Moncure Daniel. *The Writings of Thomas Paine*. 4 vols. New York: B. Franklin, 1969.
Foner, Eric. *Tom Paine and Revolutionary America*. London and New York: Oxford University Press, 1976.

"**Common Sense**": Sound judgment not based on specialized knowledge; native good judgment.

[Translation of Latin sēnsus commūnis, common feelings of humanity.]

———

Quotes:

"**Common sense** is the measure of the possible; it is composed of experience and prevision; it is calculation applied to life." [Henri Frederic Amiel]

"The philosophy of one century is the **common sense** of the next." [Henry Ward Beecher]

"**Common sense** is the knack of seeing things as they are, and doing things as they ought to be done." [Josh Billings]

"**Common sense** is only a modification of talent. Genius is an exaltation of it. The difference is, therefore, in degree, not nature." [Edward G. Bulwer-Lytton]

———

Nowadays **"common sense"** generally refers to practical attitudes and widely accepted beliefs that may be hard to justify but which are generally assumed to be reliable. Extreme deviations from common-sense beliefs may be evidence of psychological disturbance, but may, on the other hand, be the products of genius, sometimes becoming accepted later as common sense. Thus, although it is now common sense that the earth is round, only a few centuries ago a man believing this might have been regarded as mad.

———

Setting the Stage:

Well, as we all know now, the world is not flat anymore! And we are no longer fighting the British, as was Thomas Paine in 1776. The "madness and folly" to which he was referring, however, is still very present, albeit in a different form. This madness is no longer referring to an external culprit, the British monarchy and the ensuing folly of stewardship from the other side of the Atlantic Ocean.

Today, over two hundred and thirty years later, we have our own home-grown follies. Many of these have come about in incremental, evolutionary steps, and as with many changes, have gone largely unnoticed by the ones living in the here and now.

This book attempts to take a look from the inside of the United States of America at what it looks like from the outside, using not abstract philosophy but commonplace language and references to well known and ordinary customs and behaviors. The purpose is to initiate a debate about many of the conflicting and at times divisive practices that seem to have removed the concepts of common sense from public and private discourse.

America is a democratic society and its citizens still enjoy a high level of personal freedom. But since this society is also becoming more complex and multicultural, the task of honoring personal freedom while maintaining the fabric of society is turning out to be the challenge of the future.

Some of the topics that will be addressed in one way or another in this book in terms of **common sense** are:

- Rights of the individual versus rights of everyone else (society)
- Does a woman's right extend to her body?
- Focus on education, especially science and engineering
- Political paralysis: partisanship as a weapon
- Assimilation of (legal) immigrants without the loss of ethnicity
- Health of the nation-the *whole* nation
- Energy sources-safe and green
- Illegal + immigration = illegal immigration
- Politics fueled not by good intentions but by money

When wise men stay silent, stupidity reigns. [Common sense]

Common sense

(An Outsider's Look from the Inside)
How do you fit a round peg into a square hole?

1. You don't. (The realist)
2. You force it. (The dreamer)
3. You make the hole bigger. (The entrepreneur)

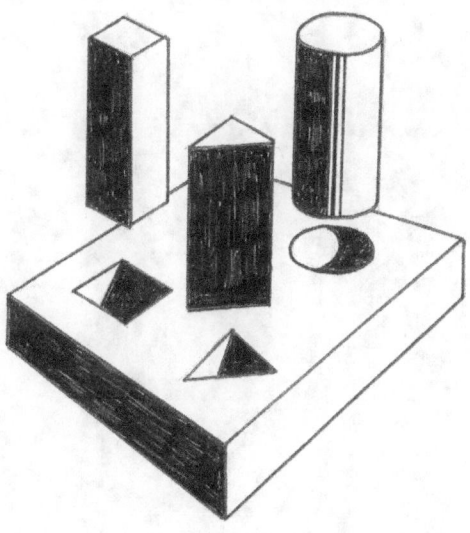

CHAPTER 1

United (?) States

THE UNITED STATES of America is in danger of becoming the Chaotic States of America. The experiment that started with the fusion of different immigrating nationalities into a homogeneous, albeit multicultural, unity, also referred to as the "melting pot," still seems to be undergoing some severe growing pains.

It is a sad state of affairs when the "greatest country" on earth (as it is still being called by Americans) is run by people who don't even believe in evolution, global warming or the importance of cooperation and compromise. It is not too worrisome, that we do have a lot of ignorant people, even in important positions - we've always had that, but it is deeply concerning that they wield so much power. We are reminded of the old saying that, "bad things happen when good people do nothing". So, we will always have the fringes, but the sensible middle majority must stand up and be counted. If not, we will lose as a civilization. We have so many REALLY important issues, which need to be addressed; infrastructure, schools, inequality and poverty, balance of power, money in politics, our role in the world etc. etc. - and sadly it does not look like the political will is there to even talk about these issues. The important discourse which was so fundamental for a well functioning democracy in its birthplace, the old Greece is slowly being strangled by special interests and an oblivious electorate.

When one looks back through history and considers the rise and fall of great nations, there seems to be one common denominator leading to the eventual erosion of power and the decline and fall of the nation or empire.

The forces at work during the rise of power, expansion and wealth were the same forces that eventually led to the demise and downfall of the nation. The ascent was fueled by curiosity, strong-minded citizens, and a willingness to sacrifice one's own situation for the common good. There was a feeling amongst common people of the presence of adventure coupled with a conviction that great things could be accomplished when working together. There was an intoxicating endorphin fueled feeling of camaraderie, of belonging - much like that amongst the members of a platoon in battle. The goal was to leave the world a better place than before, to the benefit of following generations.

The basic human drives have not changed since we first evolved as a species. These drives, which are similar, if not identical, to those ever present in the animal kingdom, are based on the desire to survive and procreate-survival often meaning fighting and enduring hardship in the quest of carving out an existence.

Although the basic instincts have not waned, they have been contained behind a facade of civilized behavior, guided by rules, regulations, and laws.

As the challenges of the upward climb diminish and people achieve a certain comfort level, the "common good" concept turns into a simpler "good for me" concept. This means that the materialistic world starts to replace the more personal interactive scenario, which is essential for a collection of people working in unity. Thus the focus is now shifted to the individual. When this happens, the intangible, non-materialistic values such as consideration, empathy, and respect for other people's needs are supplanted by an egocentric and isolationist variety, where the focus is the satisfaction of each individual in the group, to the detriment of the group as a whole.

This means that the more advanced the society becomes, the larger the forces become which repel the citizens from one another-much like identical poles on a magnet. There is no longer a basic need to support one another, and society becomes fragmented and unfocused. This is akin to passengers on a cruise liner crossing the Atlantic choosing to do the journey in their own individual boats rather than enjoying the company of all the other passengers going together.

Instead of acting in the interest of the many, the citizens are increasingly acting out of self-interests. As each individual grows more and more isolated, the interaction with others turns superficial and increasingly hostile. The individual begins to view other people as competitors and contenders for their space in the world. This whole process is exacerbated in hard times. When times get tough and compassion and cooperation is most needed, many will turn away, build walls around themselves, and distance themselves from the plights of others. This results in a loss of community. Sensible discourse becomes difficult and common goals absent. It's as if society becomes unhinged, becomes torn apart at the seams. The rivets that keep the fuselage of hopes and prosperity in the air are sheared off and the once-magnificent machine falls to the ground in a thousand pieces. Instead of reaching greater heights by staying together and cooperating toward the common good, a formerly prosperous society becomes unglued and falls apart.

So the rise of the great nation of the United States, with its myriad of different peoples, took place under the umbrella of self-sacrifice, hard work, and a common desire to make life better. And now the demise is being caused by self interest, complacency, and a desire to maintain a certain lifestyle irrespective of the effect that this may have on other people. The willingness to self-sacrifice is gone.

And the priorities have changed. In stead of planning for the overall future benefit for all, we have started to be inward looking and short sighted. We do for ourselves and we do it now! As an example can be mentioned that we spend huge amounts of money for new sports stadiums while the whole country's infrastructure is getting starved for funds. A high school in Texas this year approved the construction of a new football stadium for USD 62 million. This money is being spent on Texan's favorite sport at the same time as thousands of children go to bed every night hungry and while the plight of the homeless is rapidly deteriorating. Of course infrastructure projects such as bridges, roads, trains and electrical distribution systems is not as "sexy" as say a baseball game. But whereas a game of baseball or football is not as critical to the functioning of society, as is a well-functioning highway system, it still hawks all the headlines – and the money. In a country so enamored by stars in stripes (Yankees) and all their glorious trappings, train tracks, bridge pylons and electrical switchboards are as exciting as yesterday's weather forecast. If only a publics project could be marketed and sold as a rock concert or a World's Series, our roads would be in a much better shape.

This unfortunate development is exacerbated by the proliferation of the new technological means of interaction. When impressionable young people replace human interaction in the social sphere with electronic, remote, and impersonal sound bites, they will fail to develop the interpersonal skills that all humans need to truly communicate with one another.

What happens on the playground has always been an indispensable exercise in personal development and it is a forum where you learn to come to terms with fear, disappointment, and joy. Too many times today, parents shield their young children from the lessons that they have to learn early in their lives in order to survive the much harder challenges of real life later. The children who do not learn to handle small disappointments early will be poorly equipped to handle the larger disappointments later. They also have to learn that joy and happiness can exist in the non-material world. They have to learn to appreciate the smaller things in life, such as a walk in the forest on a damp fall morning, the smell of decaying leaves, and the smile that meets you when you help someone.

The insidious proliferation of communication gadgets leaves the individual more isolated even when he or she is connected. Communication becomes mere words; meanings and personal touch are lost in the wireless world. An essential element of communicating is the facial expressions and the posture of the body. This visual component is absent when only words and speech are interchanged and the body language is muted. It takes a long time before one learns to interpret the raised eyebrows, the shrug of a shoulder or the tight lips and flailing arms. As any mime knows whole stories can be conveyed by the use of non verbal gestures. It is thus vital that the people growing up in a heavily fortified electronic interacting world also take time out for personal interactions, i.e. through interest groups, friends, sport and hobbies.

This isolation has, on the other hand, created an intense desire for the individual to be noticed—anywhere and by anyone. The astronomical number of sites for exchange of words and pictures of any kind is a testament to the lonely and disconnected existence felt by an ever-increasing number of people in this electronic world. It is almost as if one's existence has to be validated through a connection to someone – anyone. The whole "selfie" phenomenon is driven by an intense desire to be seen, noticed and accepted.

One of the results of this intensified desire to belong, to be noticed and to be revered is the formation of cult like groups (sites), where one can feel a warm and fuzzy connectivity. The common denominator of these groups is that they share the same likes and dislikes, often with a fervor akin to a religious zeal. The rules are created by the most vocal key board users and the language used is often crude, vitriolic and offensive. You are either "in" or you belong to the enemy, in which case you are fair game. The rules around which these groups congregate are not based on facts, history or precedents but on opinions, feelings and misplaced morality. As with gang codes of conduct "disrespect" is a capital offense and any attempt to reason with their world view is considered sacrilege. Hesitation in acknowledging the "new gospel" might invite disdain and you might be shamed into submission through an endless barrage of insults delivered electronically – to you and to all of your so-called friends and contacts.

So this "conformity whip" serves a different form of moral judgement than that used in the years before Twitter and Instagram. We used to be guided by the two guardians of behavior, shame and guilt. We felt guilt whenever our actions were at odds with our conscience, this having been programmed into our "hard drive" from life's early years and honed over years of living. This guilt mechanism reminds us that what we have done or said conflicts with our own belief system. No outside forces are at work here, as opposed to the case involving "shame".

Traditionally "shame" was used by society to make a person feel excluded, not a part of the group as a way of regulating that persons behavior. If you wished to be accepted and liked you made sure that you were not made ashamed by you behavior. This "shaming tactics" does not seem to work anymore, as "Shame" is often used as a stepping stone to "Fame". Outrageous and unusual behavior is now rewarded with Fame, rather than punished by Shame. These behavioral traits have been compartmentalized and promoted by groups in an effort to spread their own gospel and to more or less brainwash large swaths of people. This process has been greatly facilitated by the arrival of the powerful social media, and the speed by which ideological structures are formed and altered puts a lot of pressure on the individual. Now, rather than being shamed by society on a larger scale with well known rules, you are being excluded or included by select groups with narrow and inflexible platforms, and you have to be constantly alert not to run afoul of their agenda. Any departure from – or critique of the established norm will be punished immediately. This dangerous development makes dialogue and healthy discussions almost impossible and it threatens to fragment society even further.

One of the more serious consequences of this petrification of the U.S. version of the Tower of Babel is that voices will be silenced – not by force but by consent. We will have free speech only in theory. Many a topic will be deemed to dangerous to approach, interesting controversial speakers will be uninvited to Universities, satire will be opened up to class action suits and weighed tolerance will be a thing of the past.

When the founding fathers ensured the constitutional right to free speech they were driven by the desire to avoid overt government control on thoughts and ideas, such as had been the case in the Old World. They realized that free speech was essential for the democratic process to work. It would drive the exchange of ideas, it would help solve problems and conflicts and it would more than anything else release the collective human innovative potential of the new nation. For this individual freedom to not wreck havoc on the unifying fabric of the large melting pot of different peoples, customs and faiths it would be assumed that the freedom of speech would come with some important caveats. The more obvious one is that words should not be used to inflame or incite to violence. And you could be held liable should your utterances offend to the point of injury.

But more importantly, the right to free speech, like most rights should also carry with it an obligation. The speech should be used within the boundaries of respectful social intercourse; it should be used as an empowering tool, not as a weapon of mass destruction. We have to remind ourselves that "When anything goes – everything goes". And so it is with speech –it has to be used wisely.

It is a sign of our times when six- to seven-year-olds are completely proficient in the function and use of iPods, iPhones, and advanced computer games but totally unable to relate to other children in a meaningful way. Their isolation and single-minded inward focus make them self-centered and oblivious to the feelings and plight of others. It is often referred to as the "Me Generation."

The success of this "Me Generation" is in part owed to their parents, who have attempted, quite successfully, to compensate for the guilt of having to work away from the children, and thus leaving the formative work to someone else. They have done this by mistakenly focusing all of their attention on the child during the limited time they had together. This concentration of attention will often lead to the child feeling empowered, as if he or she were the center of the universe. The intense attention is more often than not spiked with a good dose of material gifts aimed at making the child feel loved. And furthermore, any attempt to squeeze an ounce of discipline into that precious little time together is doomed to fail.

Much to the parents' surprise, they find out later in life that instead of attention and things, they should have bestowed real love and parental discipline. They have raised a young person who thinks of him- or herself as God's gift to mankind, a person who is used to being number one and acting as number one. They have seen their father scream at the referee at the baseball game and at all the other parents at soccer practice if their child did not get the royal treatment. They have heard the teacher being reprimanded by their mother because their little one was not considered for "special" treatment.

Whenever everyone wants to get special treatment, no one does. Furthermore, the child has been conditioned to think of other playmates as competitors, thus any cordial attempt to arrive at a mutual understanding and coexistence will be judged by: "What's in it for me?"

So, how do we make sure that three hundred million "ME's" can exist together? There are some basic suggestions. Use one language, written and spoken; educate the children in basic skills; discipline with love; and make sure that the children get both mental and physical exercise, and that they play a lot with other children. There are many more, but common for all of these suggestions is that they have to be introduced early in life to be formative.

The most essential part that helps keep the "Melting Pot" from becoming the "Salad Bowl" is the use of a common language. With all the different peoples, cultures, and behavioral norms, language is what constitutes the glue that keeps society together. It is not suggested that you can only speak English. Certainly people from other countries who have, after all, been and still are an essential ingredient for making the melting pot dynamic and colorful have every right to speak their native tongue. But the official language, the one that truly unites the country, must be English. This has to be the language used in education, business, and for conducting public discourse. A country cannot survive being "bilingual."

The current state of affairs, in which one language among all the foreign languages has been introduced on par with English, does not make any sense and it may very well be an impediment to learning the language of the land. Not much has been said about the Russians, Vietnamese, Chinese, or Scandinavians, among others. Where are their languages when you are asked to press "2" for Spanish? Which button do they press?

Common sense says that new immigrants, wherever they may come from, need some tutoring and time to learn the language. But if every social interaction can still be carried out in the mother tongue, why go to the trouble of learning English? The excuse many times is that there are so many Spanish-speaking immigrants that it only makes sense to make an exception. The counter-argument can be made that it actually keeps these people from learning English. The proof is quite evident, as many Spanish-speaking immigrants who have been here three, or even ten, years still do not speak English.

There is also the argument made that you have to present all public documents, warnings, and other written material in the public domain in Spanish. This, of course, helps people procrastinate when it comes to learning to read and write the English language; it does a huge disservice to the Spanish-speaking members of society—and it costs taxpayers a lot of money.

The political argument is that there are so many Spanish-speaking immigrants in the U.S. that it is purely a practicality to also have a parallel language-apart from the fact that it serves the interests of a very large voting block. The Russian voting block is not large enough to merit interest from the powers-that-be.

But this argument goes to the crux of the matter because if one extrapolates this theory, then in a decade or so (maybe sooner) there will be a majority speaking Spanish. Is the implication then that Spanish will become the official language in the U.S.? Judging from the present duality and the failure to establish English as the official language, that may very well be the result. This development is very pervasive, but the Spanish-speaking voting block, including the thousands who do not speak English, is growing exponentially, and in the eyes of many politicians they constitute an ever-growing (and valuable) political force.

Since a common language is the glue that keeps a nation unified, it is tantamount that we make every effort to maintain a strong English language base throughout our society. We cannot have more than one official language, as surely as we cannot drive on both sides of the road. Every day we are reminded of the mayhem that can lead to.

CHAPTER 2

Debate – Fact or Fiction

WHEN, IN A fit of rage, Joe Wilson, the representative from South Carolina, raised his finger and loudly accused the president of the United States of lying, the democratic process suffered a severe blow to its soul. As pundits and talk show hosts would have it, this was just one of many accusations exchanged in a lively debate. As if interrupting the president of the United States in his address to the joint chambers of Congress could be categorized as a mere exercise of Mr. Wilson's right to free speech!

The failure of so many prominent and intelligent members of society to admit that this outburst and rude interruption of the president's important presentation was a serious breech of civil decorum and proper behavior is indeed frightening. This was, after all, not some anonymous heckler who was screaming from the stands. This was indeed a trusted representative of the people, from whom one could expect proper behavior and congressional respect for the presidency.

Therefore, when it came to a vote on condemning the behavior as having been inappropriate and unfitting for an elected member of Congress, it was surprising to see that the votes were separated along party lines.

So the members of Congress were not voting on whether Mr. Wilson had behaved badly, in which case the statistical spread of common opinions would have crossed party lines. No, Mr. Wilson's party allies had decided to "circle the wagons" politically speaking and say to the world that a member of the opposition party has every right to heckle the president, even under the special circumstances where the president was addressing the joint session.

The Republicans were, in effect, by their vote condoning the outrageous behavior of one of their own members just because he was one of their own. This does not send a very comforting signal when it comes to their impartial judgment of Americans in general, and it paints a disturbing picture of their ethical makeup.

The wider implications to the nation's respect for authority and respectful behavior could be seen immediately by the fact that so many people did not find the outburst reprehensible. The explanation given was often that this was just another example of the division and acrimony going on in Congress on a daily basis, i.e., just another form of free speech. Many people do not seem to see the distinction between a heated debate on the floor of the Senate or a critical editorial in the newspaper and what happened on this occasion. They do not understand that there is a time and a place for many interactions in life. Just as you do not interrupt a sermon or a wedding ceremony, you do not interrupt the president of the United States when he is given the floor in Congress.

Yes, we enjoy free speech in our society, but it comes with the stipulation that it be handled responsibly. The founding fathers understood that without a free exchange of ideas and opinions, there would not be a free people. And without it we would not be able to advance society through discussion and implementation of ideas. It is, however, up to the individual to understand that the power of being able to speak freely comes with the responsibility of using this power wisely. The analogy is the power of a scalpel. It can be used for life-saving surgery-or it can be used for taking a life. It is, however, the same instrument.

The nature of public debate is also very important. There is the present danger that infomercials, sound bites, fundamentalist religion, and ideological rigidity will impair any thoughtful deliberations about national policies. You could say that the discourse will come to rest at its lowest common denominator.

Unfortunately for the country, a reasonable decorum in public debates seems to no longer be the preferred mode. During the health care debate, accusations of wanting to form death squads, or of being racist, communist, or even worse were blown into the airwaves with absolutely no reasoning and with total disregard for any damage that, in the end, this would have for the democratic process. Hotheads who have absolutely no concept of the atrocities that went on during the Third Reich even went so far as to label candidates "Nazis." This ought to be a serious affront to everyone who suffered one way or another under Hitler's reign.

In this new electronic news age with Twitter, Wikipedia and fast talking talk show hosts the unfortunate victim is the truth. The truth is changing like a chameleon changes colors depending on the surroundings. And when the truth is based on verifiable facts, those facts are questioned. This is especially true in politics where think tanks and research organizations are "molding the facts to fit the mold". Huge studies are being conducted in order to verify a specific position, be it in taxation, housing, social services or foreign policy. By thus establishing the result even before the study is commenced is of course convenient as the model and the variables are already known entities. The fact that the facts are wrong does not seem to bother too many. In the end the final decision will depend on who has the most money and who talks the loudest. The sad part of this is that the facts seldom lie. The value of the gravitational force has remained unchanged for years, the speed of light is well known, the strength of steel and cast iron can be accurately determined and the aerodynamic forces acting on an airplane in flight can be precisely ascertained.

So, what is happening when debates are taking place on serious issues such as the ones being brought forth during presidential debates leading up to an election? One side claims that there's no evidence supporting the claim that global warming is happening. The other side presents proofs in the form of analysis, photographs and lengthy reports from respected researchers that global warming is indeed happening. The other party faced with indisputable facts decides to ignore those saying that these facts are erroneous as they do not agree with that party's world view. At this point in the conversation the discussion has turned from being based on truths to being base on beliefs. The victim is the truth. One can only be thankful that airplanes, medical equipment and tall skyscrapers are not built on faith but on facts.

The founding fathers certainly did not wish public debate to be converted into a verbal sewer and they would have been mortified had they heard only a fraction of what "talking heads," talk show hosts, and political action committees are calling public discourse.

A grotesque twist to this lack of restraint and civility for some is the fact that serious constraint is applied to others under the guise of "political correctness" (PC). As much as derogatory talk is permitted-even accepted-when it comes from certain sources, there are some subjects that have been deemed heretic and un-PC by these same sources. It is therefore safe to say that "free speech" only applies to accepted topics, the ones that do not offend anyone-or just some select media outlets?

"Anyone" is, in reality, a lot of people and it can sometimes be difficult to find out what someone finds offensive. This purge of questionably offensive speech by self-established "word police" is almost akin to the attempted purge of alleged communists in the McCarthy era. So, maybe "free speech" in the U.S. today is not so free anymore. One person who found that out the hard way was Helen Thomas, long-time member of the White House Press Corps. She spoke of a subject matter considered taboo by some-and was consequently forced to take early retirement.

Common sense says that if we want to preserve the democratic model for our nation, we have to first reinstate a proper decorum for public discourse. We can have our differences with respect to the severity of problems and to the nature of solutions; however, we have to be able to discuss these openly and without resorting to damaging and personal rhetoric. If we fail to do so, we will have obliterated the most powerful democratic tool in our arsenal: free speech.

ELECTRONIC ESCALATION

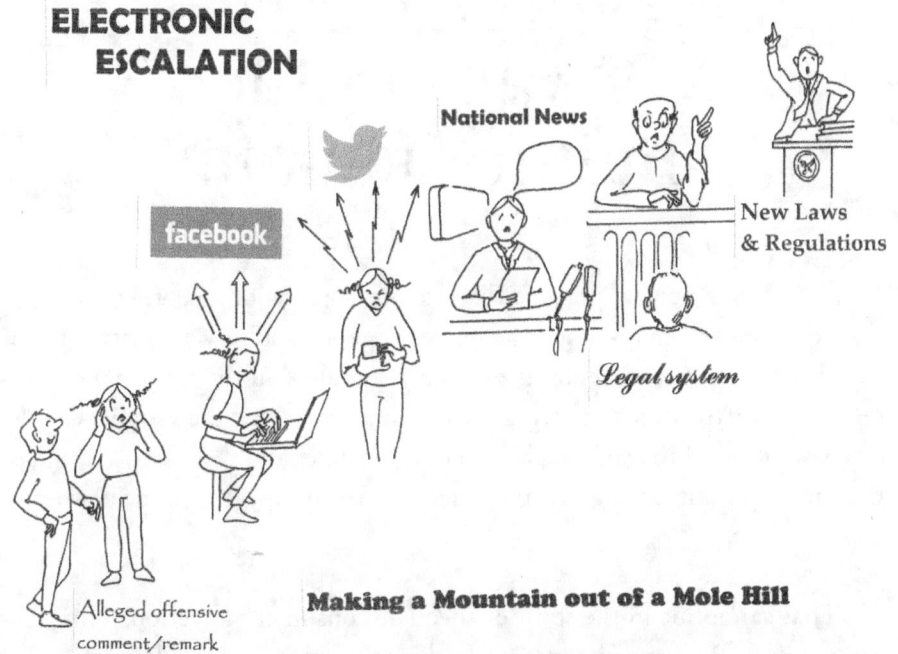

National News

New Laws & Regulations

Legal system

Alleged offensive comment/remark

Making a Mountain out of a Mole Hill

CHAPTER 3

Privacy in the Public Domain

IT HAS BECOME normal practice that the burden for not accepting the terms and conditions from a vendor or supplier of goods and services rests with the consumer. This phenomenon is especially prevalent in the financial services sector, with credit cards, mortgages, etc. This means that the supplier can decide new terms of the contract between the supplier and the client, and unless the client opts out, usually within a predetermined time frame, the new terms go into effect.

That cannot be in the spirit of adequate consumer protection! This is almost akin to finding someone in your living room before you have extended an invitation to that person to enter. So what gives someone the right to sign you up for a service just because you failed to let them know that you did not want that service in the first place? This seems to be the horse before the cart, and it is a practice that can have serious repercussions.

Usually a contract of goods and services has to be presented to the buyer, and customarily an acceptable sales agreement is presented for the buyer to sign. Failure to sign the contract, of course, makes the deal null and void.

It is only common sense that the basic contract is the default, and that any additions have to be approved by the client/customer.

Even Facebook has been questioned about its practice of having an open profile as the default. It has been suggested that only family and friends should be in the initial loop as the basic default setting, and that the user would have to actively request that this be widened, whenever he or she desires to do so. Is that not also common sense?

If it were only possible to opt out of receiving junk mail!

With the proliferation of electronic interaction and the development of super algorithms we have now arrived at a juncture in the world of private and personal security, where we are no longer in charge of what and which part of our lives is collected, analyzed and disseminated. All the information which exists on the web about our person, our past and our connections has been mined by companies who are interested in either selling us something or stealing something from us. We are being categorized, labeled and evaluated; our likes, preferences, phobias, waste size, medical records and reading material are all being swept up together with our credit card numbers, birthday and wife's social security numbers. And with the powerful and fast computer program processes any grouping and targeting can be produced from which can be engineered strategies and action plans.

This is very intrusive and an affront to any privacy laws, however we have not yet devised methods for protecting bits of information which exists in the public realm. Before, your medical records were in the form of paper filed in folders in suitable cabinets. These cabinets could be locked and only authorized personnel would have access. There were strict guidelines and rules for who could access and what could be done with the sensitive information.

Now, the information, be it text or pictures is in a digitized format floating in the Cloud, accessible for anyone who can hack the security system. What makes this system even more vulnerable to data mining is the volume of information each person accumulates through his or her lifetime. You cannot apply for a membership or go to the doctor or dentist without having to publicize yet again all the facts and figures about your person, family and relationships. Even the most secret personal identifier, your social security number is required on many non-essential documents.

You can have a medical operation refused, without knowing it was because the hospital obtained a secret report that listed you as unlikely to pay. A college can turn your application down because they suspected you were unlikely to complete four years of payment. Or you didn't get a job because of a report unknown to you listed you as a possible drug addict. In neither of those instances are you aware of what has happened to your name and reputation.

The best way of avoiding that personal and private information becomes available is to make sure that it does not exist in an electronic format. The prudent advise, especially to young people who are so enamored with being seen and heard, is to tell them that they should never communicate in private on electronic media what they do not want for everyone in the world to see and hear.

As the line goes when the police reads a suspected perpetrator of a crime his or her rights, "Everything that you say may be used against you!" The safe thing is to say nothing.

CHAPTER 4

Politicians - Serving Whom?

Is IT NOT strange that a person who has worked hard and diligently toward obtaining his life's calling-that of serving society by becoming a politician-is less focused on implementing changes and improvements once he has arrived at the destination and is more concerned about maintaining his position as a politician?

Your whole life you have aspired to get to the place and position where you could make a difference. And then, when you get there, you find that getting the things done for which your heart was on fire could cost you your reelection.

Was the cost of the journey worth it? Your investments have not paid any dividend for the American people, your constituents. But then, on the other hand, you have been greatly rewarded financially for just being there. And the lifestyle is certainly one you and your family could get used to quite quickly.

Your convictions have been replaced by donations and you place your vote out of fear of being replaced.

This is especially evident in an election year. Well, the new election campaign starts right after the old one has concluded, so we can almost refer to the "never-ending" election campaign for the seat holder, be it a member of Congress or the American President. This in effect means that the politician is reminded throughout his tenure that whatever he says or does shall be measured in terms of what it does to his re-election. In stead of thus making statements, decisions and proposals in line with his belief system, he is forced to behave as if the electorate is looking over his shoulder at every twist and turn. In other words, in stead of acting with the powers vested in him by his voters and in accordance with his own core beliefs, he will have to navigate the period between elections using an imaginary and elusive "public opinion" polling scale. As Thomas Friedman, the syndicated columnist once said, "When everyone is so busy running, is it any surprise that no one is running the federal government?"

The result, as we have witnessed during the last campaign has been that none of the presidential contenders have had the guts to state their firm opinions on the challenges facing this nation. Rather than making the serious (serious for them) mistake of saying something which could be interpreted as a position on a certain issue, they have elected to say nothing – with the result that none of the critical issues have been debated. All the air time has been allocated, eaten up, devoured by non-essential personal attacks and frivolous accusations.

This is like a bad rendition of Hans Christian Andersen's "The Emperor's new Suit", where none of the politicians up for election at the same time as the Presidential election dare state the obvious, namely that the presidential candidate of their party may be completely unfit to fill the job. They are all scared and hiding behind an imaginary wall of denial. This is another dangerous case of, "bad things happen when good people say nothing!"

But, of course their jobs are at stake! As if that would be more important than taking a stand and trying to save the jobs of millions. Where are the politicians with convictions and the guts to stand by them? These men of principles are all the more required in todays' fast moving climate of technology changes, environmental challenges, human displacements and ethical issues – all coming at you almost at the speed of light. It is vital that the political leaders and heads of industry have a firm grasp of the fundamentals and the core principles. Only then will they be able to chart the course for the future with all its unforeseen derivations and complicated algorithms. This is akin to the captain of a ship who knows where he is going and knows how to read the charts – he still has to constantly plot his position and a new course.

Being responsible to the American people is no longer your priority, even though you often claim to act on their behalf. You have sold your soul to the highest bidder, and now your lifestyle prohibits you from doing what you actually came there to do. So, how do feel about it? Well by now you have probably internalized your "civic spirit" to believe that you are doing society a service.

Why can't a well-meaning politician be elected for the cause he believes in and then go all-out to have that change implemented in the parliamentary way? Forget about being reelected. He did not get the job in the first place to get reelected; he did it to carry out a mission in which he believed. So, "get in-do good-and get out."

We have to be very careful. Just because the political process in Washington is gridlocked and our trust in the appointed representatives is at an all-time low, we should not "throw the baby out with the bath water". I understand the frustration and the anger over the disenfranchisement of the ordinary citizens, where all the power, money and influence are concentrated with the few. But there is no easy fix. Unfortunately many Americans have been influenced by the entertainment industry, be it movies, sports or television where complicated problems are either easily solved or ridiculed as being – too complicated.

With the notable exception of Sen. Rand Paul and Gov. John Kasich one of the Republican debate on CNN felt like the annual meeting of the "Dr. Strangelove" society. They seemed to want to solve the world's problems by bombing everyone, who is not on the side of the red-white and blue. Some of them, like the fire-breathing Fiorina would not ever want to talk to her adversaries. Bombs – not words. This is indeed scary. Don't they realize that the world has changed since the Second World War? And the debate was held in the Ronald Reagan Library, in honor of the great communicator, who was not afraid of having a dialogue with his adversaries, be they Gorbachev or Tip O'Neil. And there we have the candidates for US Commander in Chief spewing hatred and threats of war. I hope the American people will be able to use some common sense in this "New World" of ours. We cannot defeat our terrorist adversaries militarily. You cannot shoot an idea or bomb an ideology.

So, the republican front runner is a billionaire "man of the people" and he seemingly has quick fixes to many of the country's serious challenges. He has struck the cords of dissatisfaction, anger and fear in a non-PC manner, which appeals to the masses. But, can he govern? Politics is the art of the possible and governing is not the same as running a large corporation. Governing requires showing respect towards your adversaries, having the ability to compromise in the interest of all of the people and possessing a lot of patience in seeking possible solutions. So far the republican front runner has shown none of those traits.

He is riding a wave of popular sentiment, as if the electoral process were a reality show or the Super Bowl. I think we have to be careful with what we wish for – we just might get it

There are other disturbing facts about how the time in Washington is being spent. Apart from politicians allocating most of their time to making sure that they can be reelected, there is also the question of working for the whole of the country. One has the strong feeling at times, especially at federal budgeting time, that the nation as a whole is superseded by each individual lawmaker's home state. It is time to "bring home the bacon." If the senator would not be so hell-bent on being reelected, maybe he could then look at the big picture. Instead he puts on his state's blinders and concentrates on getting as much "pork" as possible back to his home state, even if that pork is only money and would never pass a cost-benefit test.

That's not all. When he is forced to look at the big picture and work on long-term planning for the benefit of the nation, his opinions are often skewed by the party machine's food processor. Party politics often trump individual initiative and innovative thinking.

Alas, not all is lost. When he finally does leave his office with its position and perks, he walks right across the street, or a little further, to Crystal City, where he picks up a cushy, well-paid job as counselor or consultant to one of the companies with whom he has been enjoying a rather cozy relationship in his former job.

When Harry Truman, after leaving the Oval Office, was asked why he would not take such a job, his simple and common-sense response was, "You don't want me. You want my position and my contacts-and I no longer have these to offer."

Many large corporations have anti-competitive clauses built in to their employment contracts with people in management and executive positions. This is, of course, to avoid the kind of industrial espionage that could rise out of these people bringing with them invaluable secrets to serve their new employer-the competitor. This, by the way, also applies to chief analysts and systems specialists now that a lot of a company's product and marketing secrets are harbored on the company's host computer in an electronic format.

This simple, common-sense approach could also be applied to government employees, some of whom control very large taxpayer-sponsored projects and budgets. There is an inherent suspicion of the impartiality of a government buyer's decision when that same buyer, after ending his "public service" with the government, could be employed by a company vying for these contracts. The practical, albeit unethical, way in which many high-powered government employees get around the appearance of impropriety is by continuing as consultants or by joining one of the multitude of legal firms lining every government building in Washington, D.C. This artificial "arm's length activity" seems to be an accepted way of continuing one's working career. It should also be added that these "retired" managers usually receive much larger salaries, and most likely bonuses, in their new employ.

So whereas ordinary students have to pay for their college tuition, these "students of government" get theirs paid for by the taxpayer. And they have a job lined up long before they "graduate" and enter the private sector.

Maybe we need to get back to the original premise of public service, in which elected officials serve in Washington, D.C. for a limited period, after which they return to their former occupations. They should at least not be allowed to join the private sector in the same field in which they were involved as politicians.

In addition to making the whole procurement system more transparent, this would also have two other benefits: first, that it would enable a lot more bright and enthusiastic people to serve their country in Washington, D.C., and, secondly, it would infuse the home states and cities with servants who would thus be the wiser for having seen the "other side" of the art of governing this great country. This could lead to a whole new awareness of the art of politics for the people. As it is now, it is safe to say that it does not work. There are career politicians who would have to be pried out of the woodwork if they were made to leave.

As stated before, their duty seems not to be toward serving the country, although they keep reminding everyone that they speak for their constituency. No, their duty seems to be toward continuing their stay. What seems to have happened is that apart from being masters in their own limited universe, most of them have lost touch with the real world.

These career politicians have no idea what Americans go through when they lose their job, their house, or their medical coverage. They see their primary job as that of bringing as much business to their state as possible irrespective of the value and consequence to the country as a whole. The Balkanization of the country starts inside the Beltway; it is therefore no wonder that the country outside the Beltway suffers.

Many citizens do not realize that members of Congress constitute a kind of ruling or privileged class of exactly the type our founding fathers were set against. Members of Congress under the Constitution enjoy the privilege of being free from arrest in all cases except for treason, felony, and breach of the peace. Congress has also been criticized for awarding themselves higher salaries by slipping these into a large bill at the last minute. And it is rumored that they have plans to excuse themselves from abiding by the effects of the healthcare reform.

Reports also abound of lavish trips abroad at taxpayers' expense. One of these trips included spas, three-hundred-dollars-per-night extra, unused rooms, shopping, excursions, tours of historic buildings, fancy dinners, escorts by military officials, and free flights courtesy of the Air Force.

Why would a hardworking machinist in Toledo, Ohio, pay for a gourmet dinner for his representative and friends at an expensive restaurant abroad, when he himself can hardly even afford to feed his kids? Common sense tells the taxpayer that this lavish expense serves only one purpose-and that this was not the reason for sending his congressman to Washington, D.C.

CHAPTER 5

Education-A Golden Opportunity

MOST CHILDREN AROUND the world would give their right arm in order to get a proper education-or any education, for that matter. In large parts of the world an education is the only ticket out of hopelessness and poverty, and not having even the opportunity to study and learn leaves them in the barren desert of ignorance and despair-and, worse, with no hope.

Also, most, if not all, young people want to learn. You see it already right after they have entered this world, exploring that world first with their mouths, then with their fingers, and lastly with their brains. There is nothing more amazing than a three-year-old child who is learning the power of words. Their brains are like black holes consuming all the new words and trying them on for size constantly, even sometimes to the point where they are driving their parents mad with the repetitiveness. Leaving children on their own with all kinds of odd-shaped blocks, pins, balls, and rocks will bring out their budding curiosity about forms, shapes, and constructions, which will eventually lead them to the level and capacity of non-material and imaginary thinking. This is a normal process that can only be halted and altered by their surroundings. Nature has created the curious child; nurture can further or retard the learning process.

In discussions of human rights, it is often mistakenly postulated that all children are created equal. This is, of course, not true as genetics has a decisive influence on the future capabilities and abilities of the new arrival. What is true, though, is that all children should be given the chance to fully develop their potential both as functioning human beings and as members of society. Proper education is the "brick and mortar" in their future "house of existence." The obligation to provide proper education to children is therefore one of the most important ones for all governments and societies around the world.

A country's education is only as good as its teachers; good teachers are priceless. Can we afford not to regard the education of our children as "price-less"? Being a teacher ought to be more attractive than being a lawyer and should also be rewarded accordingly.

In the industrialized world, access to schools and other learning centers has improved greatly over the last century, and there are even countries where schooling is free, paid for by the government.

Unfortunately, not all places in the world are financially equipped yet to cover the educational requirements after they have spent the necessary money for food, housing, and emergency medical coverage. The irony here is that while these countries are genuinely struggling to allocate funds for education, some of the wealthier countries suffer from an almost opposite set of challenges. In these countries where the educational apparatus is readily available and enjoys a relatively high standard, an increasing number of children are strangely disinterested in going to school.

In some developed countries, it is almost as if learning has become a chore, not an opportunity. Apart from discounting that learning can lead to a better and more secure life, the personal pride and satisfaction of studying and of learning a topic and/or a trade has disappeared from the core family value system. This is in great part driven by the prevalent culture of instant gratification and absence of traditional family values. In cultures where learning is revered and intelligence and ability rewarded, there is a great deal of personal pride in achieving higher levels of learning, not only for the resulting earning power but more for the feeling of self-satisfaction and accomplishment by the individual.

Learning and the desire to learn normally start in the family and at a young age. This latent desire is fairly strong and not limited by place and time. As the child grows older, roadblocks can get in the way in the form of economic impediments, parental reluctance, or lack of interest.

As an example of economic barriers, many children in developing countries do not have a chance to complete their basic education. They are taken out of school to help farm the land or assist in the survival of the family in other ways. And often, should they be lucky enough to complete the basic schooling period, they will then not be given the opportunity to further their education since their family cannot afford the books or the transportation to school. These kids are considered instant revenue generators and the family cannot wait until they would have increased their earning power through higher education. This is an evil cycle being kept in place by ignorance and poverty.

The parental impediment to the children learning is just as disruptive to the process as poverty itself. This is caused by parents either not understanding or having an appreciation for the value of education, or by their not being able to assist their children with reading and homework. The former is much more disruptive than the latter because it helps dissuade the children from taking an active part in the learning process. This means that parents who themselves disliked the learning experienced or hated school for whatever reason will send the wrong message to their own children about the quality and value of education.

The disruptive cycle of non-education is hard to break as it becomes institutionalized and passed down with the family culture. It almost becomes genetic. This is where good teachers can do miracles. Through attentiveness to the child's family difficulties and appreciation of the desire to learn, they can indeed "light the fire of discovery" for the personal exploits of that child.

Then there are the children whose only impediment to the learning process is that they do not see the benefits of learning, at least not in the traditional sense. They feel that they have inherited a right to a good income and an interesting job just by being. They feel entitled to a good place in society, but they are not prepared to sweat for it. They have taken note of all the marketing messages, the gist of which in most cases is that the enjoyment of life is an effortless endeavor and it comes at a prepaid price, courtesy of their parents. They have come to believe in "instant gratification." They have not been taught that "fruits come from labor" and that any worthwhile achievement comes as a result of having expended a personal effort. They do not realize that the sports stars they so admire have advanced to their height through sweat and bodily pain. They fail to see that a successful mechanic, carpenter, plumber, etc. has earned a trade that has been honed and perfected over years. It did not "just come" all by itself.

It is only by negotiating the road of life that one gets to appreciate the miles covered. Ethics and Common Sense should be taught in high schools across the country. Together with banking, investing, budgeting, balancing a check book, consumer protection, mortgage contracts, responsible sex, child rearing, dispute resolution, etc.

These skills combined with an ethical attitude and a good arsenal of common sense tools should ensure that the new young citizen is well equipped to handle life's challenges and to enjoy its rewards

In the new competitive global workplace, we in the U.S. still need plumbers and carpenters, but we should re-tool our educational system to meet the fierce challenges facing us. We have to work smarter-but that also entails that we become smarter. Most of our kinetic energy driving this country forward is not generated by educating more liberal-arts majors, lawyers, or even Wall Street whizzes. No, it will come from raising the quantity and quality of science and engineering graduates as well as good and skilled craftsmen. Common sense tells us that our scientific and technological edge can be lost very easily if we do not turn out or import a lot more engineers and scientists. Any edge or privilege lost in the technical realm may not be easily regained. America is already losing manufacturing jobs to other countries where the wages are lower and smart workers are available. We have to ensure that the flight of brawn is not followed by the flight of brains.

On a more basic level, we have to find a way to open up our young people's eyes for the "blood, sweat, and tears" worth of putting in an honest day's work. Many young people are disillusioned, lazy, and idle, and they need a real-world wake up call that can get their attention. One way would be to create a nationwide draft for all young people for a year, during which they would be working with communal projects, assistance to the poor and elderly, and other public works. This "boot camp" would help them get some structure in their life, as well as showing them that they can indeed make a difference and helping themselves helping others.

Another way of enlightening them to the value of work would be to send them to some village in the developing world to help out with specific tasks. This method is already being used in Germany. They have started a pilot project in which they send troubled youngsters to remote towns in Siberia, where they experience hardship, learn respect for others, and regain pride in their own accomplishments.

And maybe there should be paid more attention to vocational education. The country after all needs more than just liberal arts and political science majors. Even though our society is becoming more and more dependent on electronic systems and computerized infrastructure, we still need people who can service the most basic parts of these systems. Young people with a flair for the practical side of life should not have to spend years in college immersed with theoretical learnings. We have almost reached the point where you are not qualified for any job unless you have a college diploma. This needs to change lest we end up with too many unemployable and unfulfilled graduates who could have been much more productive and happy elsewhere.

One rather unique feature in the American learning universe is the fact that sports play such a big role. The ancient Greeks knew that a sound mind thrives best in a sound body, and they always made sure that physical exercise was a part of the young people's schooling. *A part of*-not substituting it! In American schools, the physical part of the "whole body" experience is often displacing or replacing the part where the mind is being exercised

The ability to play any sports in school is often looked upon by the school as a very valuable commodity for the benefit of the school itself. Whereas the school should serve the student by giving him or her universal learning skills in order for that person to be able to get ahead in life and be a good, contributing citizen, the student is now serving the school by using their skills and time in the service of the football team, the field hockey team, etc. By playing on the person's natural abilities as a sportsman, the school is giving the student what he wants, such as fame, fun, and friends, rather than what he needs, such as an education. Rather than being a training ground for traits such as cooperation, perseverance, and honesty, the sports field becomes a refuge away from book learning and homework. It replaces that for many – not all.

Students in American universities can actually get a stipend to go to a particular university solely because of their athletic prowess. The value to the university of hiring/funding such an athlete vastly overshadows the value of the education that this student will gather during the college years. It has even been documented that these student-athletes do not have to perform to the same rigorous academic standards on tests as do other, less fit students. This gives a whole new meaning to the expression "a level playing field"!

It is correct that a few of these "student-athletes" do go on to make a living in the world of sports applying the skills they honed during their college years; some even before they graduate from the institution of higher learning. There are a couple of facts, though, that are worth noting and to which students should pay attention before embarking on this route to "lifelong" success. First, it is not lifelong and, second, it is only a tiny fraction of the very best who will eventually make a decent living from this "education."

Typically an athletic career spans ten to fifteen years, depending on how punishing to the body the sport is, whereas a good education lasts a lifetime.

As an aside, the career of many a young sports person starts on the basis of an incomplete and, at times, substandard education. High school is completed irrespective of grades, since these are not crucial to the athlete's ability to enter a good college. College is often interrupted by a draft system, which sees education only as a subterfuge, a holding pen where the future star player or athlete is being groomed for the big league. This means that many young people who have been carried through this venue to financial success in their sport have very little understanding of the world and how it works. They look upon the earth from a high pedestal, which they have not had to climb, but on which they were placed by special interests.

This "instant" adulation and access to lots of money at such a young, impressionable age can lead to the corruption of the soul, especially if the athlete has not matured in spirit.

With the money to be made in professional sports in America, it is no surprise that so many young people are attracted to becoming star athletes. However, common sense should tell them that their chances are minuscule and that while they pursue their dream, they should also bring their brain along for the ride. To get a good and safe ride in life, they need not only a good, reliable engine but also a rudder and a compass, the last one (hopefully) having been given to them by their parents at a young age.

Common sense tells us that the education of our children is tantamount to the future success of our country. Money allocated to the learning activity at all levels of our society is an investment-one we cannot afford to defer.

In support of the educational system Dwight D. Eisenhower in his book, "Crusade of Europe" in 1948 wrote, that "Once the recruit of 1941 was inducted into the service the military leader had to shoulder almost exclusive responsibility for imparting the understanding of rights and duties, but there was implied a glaring deficiency in our country's educational process. It seemed to me that constant stressing of the individual rights and privileges of American citizenship had overshadowed the equally important truth that such individualism can be sustained only so long as the citizen accepts his full responsibility for the welfare of the nation that protects him in the exercise of these rights."

This was said over 70 years ago in a different time of our history, however it still holds true.

CHAPTER 6

U.S. Foreign Policy-Doctrine

THERE HAVE BEEN numerous incidents during the life of this relatively young nation when foreign policy has been determined by a narrow mindset of special interests, often under the guise of fulfilling some higher moral objectives. One has only to mention names such as Chile's Pinochet, the Shah of Iran, Israel, and Panama. The standard excuse for rendering our support and ultimately intervening by military means is that the U.S. is trying to protect the democratic aspirations of the people-not our people, but their people. And not *their* form of democracy-ours.

Now we are at it again, this time in Iraq and Afghanistan. Once more we are giving the local population a brutal lesson in Democracy 101, in the name of humanity, self-protection, and sheer benevolence. Or so we say. Do we really know why we are there? Are we in Iraq because of some greater global strategic plan, or are we there because of our personal interests focusing on the presence of oil and the preservation of the State of Israel? Allegedly we are in Iraq because of some unsubstantiated excuse that the leader of Iraq, Saddam possessed weapons of mass destruction. To that excuse was later added that we wanted to avenge the 9/11 terror attack and to make certain that such an attack would not happen again.

Most Americans have long ago realized that they are being fed an official story, which even in the imaginations of Hollywood scriptwriters cannot possibly make any sense. However, Americans have also been led to believe that we are militarily invincible and morally superior. So what we are doing must be right. Besides, as with the Hollywood scripts, problems are usually solved with brutal force and within an allotted time frame, usually two hours and always with the "good guys" coming out on top, bruised but safe. This script, however does not work for a protracted war.

It reminds us of the old adage: "When all you have is a hammer, all the problems start looking like nails."

But, as a people, we have to ask ourselves the question about what kind of role we wish to play in the world community-and which role we can ultimately afford to play. It should be the sacred task of the administration, together with Congress representing the people, to outline a "World Constitution" specifying the policies for dealing with the world order in general.

The notion that the American people can live isolated from the rest of the world is plainly wrong in this day and age, and it will simply be ludicrous to behave as if our actions and the actions of others will not have impacts far beyond the national borders.

Equally wrong is the notion that we are supreme beings and that we—and only we—have the recipe for a moral and just society. We often claim that the U.S. is the best country in the world and therefore everyone else around the globe should be so lucky as to be able to live and behave like we do.

In an open letter in September, 2013 Vladimir V. Putin, the President of Russia in response to a speech by President Obama said the following: "I would rather disagree with a case he made on American exceptionalism, stating that the United States' policy is "what makes America different. It's what makes us exceptional." It is extremely dangerous to encourage people to see themselves as exceptional, whatever the motivation. There are big countries and small countries, rich and poor, those with long democratic traditions and those still finding their way to democracy. Their policies differ too. We are all different, but when we ask for the lord's blessings, we must not forget that God created us equal."

Well, for starters, there are a lot of people, maybe millions, residing in the United States who do not share the feeling of being fortunate living here, as they are having a tough time finding and enjoying the "freedom" and "prosperity" in this type of democracy. Likewise, there are a lot of places in the world where people are just as happy, or more so, with their type of democracy and their way of life. Who's to say that a retired Frenchman sitting, reading the newspaper, and having an aperitif at his local café is not just as happy as a New York accountant going through tomorrow's work on his two-hour train ride back to his town house in New Jersey? For starters, the Frenchman does not have to worry about affording the cost of health care. And he still reserves his inalienable rights to love his country and to criticize any current government.

There are a lot of different ways of preparing a chicken for the dinner table. And there are a lot of different spices and herbs available around the world to make the dish unique and delicious. And so it is with living. There are a lot of different ways of living and enjoying life. The family sitting on the floor in a Thai village gathered around the multitude of shared dishes while joking and laughing about the day's events enjoys life just as much as a couple in San Francisco staring lovingly at each other across a candlelit table while enjoying a good bottle of vintage Merlot from nearby Napa Valley.

So why this deeply set desire to solve other people's alleged societal problems? Why not be cognizant of the fact that a square peg does not fit in a round hole-or that there are other, well-functioning societies that are different from ours? There is no doubt that we can all learn from each other, and we can most assuredly find some aspects of other societies and ways of life that could enhance our own. But we must start with the respect for and understanding of why these differences are there-or maybe just the recognition that they are there.

So, when the American government condemns practices conducted elsewhere in the world, it should be with the understanding that these practices be judged not solely on an American norm, but on a wider humanitarian basis, respecting the laws and practices of the country in question. We are, of course, not talking about acts of genocide and other such atrocities, which would quite categorically be deemed a humanitarian issue. In such cases, it is the duty of every nation on earth to intervene and stop such acts.

In conclusion, it would therefore be advisable that the United States of America embark on a different set of foreign policy doctrines based on understanding and compassion, not fear. To be compassionate does not mean being weak. The safer the world is for all, the safer it will be for the few-the U.S. included.

"We Build Better Weapons for Peace."
(General Dynamics)

CHAPTER 7

Earmarks and Elections

IT IS WELL known that state and federal programs shall be opened to the fair, free market through a public bidding process. After all, these programs are funded by taxpayers. The rules for submitting the bids are well defined in documentation outlining the technical and performance criteria, as well as the contractual and financial requirements. To keep the bidders honest and the evaluation fair, the bids are almost always sealed and they are to be opened under the watchful eyes of an impartial group. This group will subsequently validate the bids and if they meet the criteria of the bid specifications, the best bid shall be chosen for the contract. This could be based either on lowest price or best value.

The bid documents generally outline the rules for selection of the awarded party, such as lowest initial cost, lowest lifetime costs with a defined time line, the ability to support the program logistically over time, or-as has now become a valued parameter-the lowest cost with the smallest environmental footprint. There may be other criteria for the selection, but common in all of these is that they shall be known before the bids are submitted; they have to be a part of the bid formulation. Only then does the state or federal contractor have assurances that the bids reflect the actual execution of the specific contract.

This is the way it should be, predictable and fair. Only when this is the case and there is full transparency can suppliers and entrepreneurs plan their R&D programs and predict reasonable and viable production budgets.

The real world as concerns state and federal bids, however, is a far cry from this. Bids are often rewarded without a bidding process to companies that have in some way or other supported a certain political party or individual lawmaker. These awards are often referred to as "earmarks"-federal dollars that lawmakers direct to special persons or companies.

It's not supposed to work that way. For instance, federal law requires that all military contracts, even "earmarks," be offered through competitive bidding. Exceptions are allowed in those few cases where the military has an urgent need or the product is unique.

As an example of how this policy of earmarking skews the competitive climate through unfair practices, there is the case of a Sammamish, Washington, based entrepreneur who sells the army's elite special forces T-shirts that resist burning-a feature that can save the lives of soldiers under fire. He wanted to sell his creation to the marines, as well. This entrepreneur worked for months to prepare the bid and was very stunned to learn that another company was awarded the t-shirt contracts without having had to compete. The other company in question had lobbied members of Congress for an "earmark."

The lobbying worked, despite a flaw with the other company's synthetic t-shirt. It melts to the skin under intense heat, causing serious burns. As a result, marines are forbidden to wear the shirts in combat. This material fact was a direct violation of the technical requirements of the bid.

The Sammamish-based entrepreneur argued that handing the business over to one company favored by Congress robs the process of all integrity. "I spent forty years of my life doing it the way you're supposed to do it," he said. "Do it the competitive way, so that everybody wins."

This is apparently not the way that people in Congress are looking at it. They're supposed to be protectors of the powers of free enterprise and a fair and free market; however, when it comes to public and fair bidding in their home state, their willingness to play by the rules is often victim to the forces of financial gains. They call it self-preservation in political terms; everybody else calls it selfish and inexcusable. In the long term, it is also very destructive for the competitiveness in the American workplace. When the work goes where the senator wants it to go, rather than where it could be most efficiently and effectively done, the senator is in effect robbing the marketplace to feed his own political aspirations. And the taxpayers' money is taken hostage.

Were this practiced in a third world country, we would label it "corruption." Here, we call it "pork," "special interests," or "politics as usual"!

We have created a monster, like in the movie *Little Shop of Horrors*, where the plant Audrey II thrives on blood from its caretaker, Seymour. As it gets bigger and more demanding ("Feed me!"), the situation gets out of control. Audrey II is finally electrocuted and dies, so the movie has a happy ending. There are certain unmistakable similarities to our democratic electoral system. Instead of "blood," we are talking about "money," the difference here for some people being minuscule. And there is no happy ending.

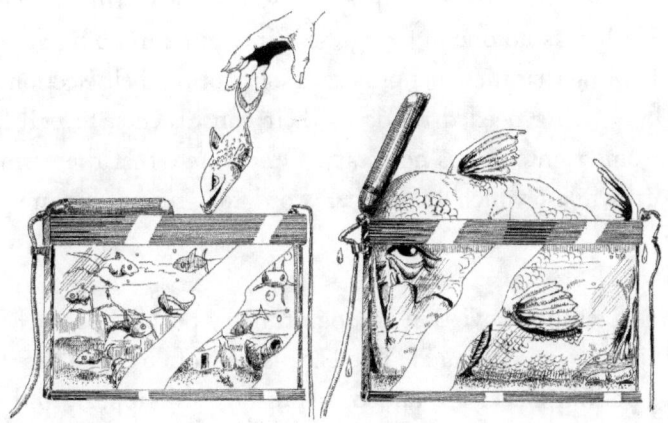

Nowhere in the world is so much money being spent in the electoral processes as in the U.S. It is no longer enough to want to do good and serve your country-you also have to be flush. There is a saying, "We have the best government money can buy." So if you are an enthusiastic, bright person who wishes to climb the political ladder, through the city to the state level and finally to

Congress, you have to amass an incredibly large war chest, which means you have to have a lot of willing donors. Some of these donors are quite rich and powerful, and the suspicion here is that they may want to have a *quid pro quo* arrangement, at least in spirit, should you get elected.

This is where ethics enters the equation. Assuming that the donors gave financial help to this particular senator because they agreed with his principles and voting record, there should be no outside pressure on him not to proceed with his program. However, they may still exert pressure on him from time to time when their interests could be furthered or jeopardized. The senator should not be swayed and should stick to his convictions and his agenda; in other words, he should not confuse the objective of his job with that of his reelection campaign.

This gets us to the "earmarks process," a procedure where lawmakers insert language that gets federal funds for pet projects back home, often referred to as "pork." Attempts have been made from time to time to change this procedure. Whereas no one in Congress is interested in doing away with the practice, claiming that these pet projects are honoring their election campaign promises by proving needed funds to their constituents, several lawmakers agree that some tightening is necessary. Others state that the earmarks need to be "worthwhile," which is another word for "supporting my reelection campaign."

There is a strong conviction among ordinary people in the U.S. that the whole election process is rigged. The U.S. is not, of course, a developing nation where polling places are raided, ballot boxes disappear, and donations come from the powerful with IOU's to be cashed in later – or do they?

But, as the last months of the four year presidential election session in the US winds down, the questions related to the democratic process have again been brought to the fore. We pride ourselves of being a true democracy and we never hesitate to lecture the rest of the world of the beauties of the old Greek system of "Government by the people – for the people". But do we really have a government in which the supreme power is vested in the people – all of the people?

Probably not!

First there is the amount of money spent by voters and corporations trying to influence the electoral process. With the Supreme Court case (now also commonly known as *Citizens United)* some restrictions on how corporations can spend money in elections were eliminated, leading to a tsunami of money from powerful individuals attempting to influence the election.

Then there is the practice of states deciding their own voter ID laws. The party in power can decide the rules by which the individual citizen can qualify as a valid voter. This "Eye of the needle" approach is successfully being applied in some conservative states as a means of restricting certain types of voters, usually poor and disadvantaged people from taking part in the democratic process. This way of disenfranchising eligible voters is legal however un-American and unethical.

3 VOTES   **3000 VOTES**

Another smartly devised tool for influencing the voting is the method of "Gerrymandering". This system allows the party in power to manipulate the boundaries of an electoral constituency so as to favor one party. With the use of elaborate algorithms the Gerrymandering is a highly successful tool for circumventing the democratic ideal, i.e. "stacking the deck".

And if all else fails one can put pressure on the representatives in the election, also called "Delegates". Although it is forbidden by law to influence the delegates by offering them money or jobs one can think of many other ways of "sweetening" the pot for the influential delegate – and most of these ways are being put to good and successful use during the election.

So, as can be deduced from the above we are a long way from the democratic system of "one person, one vote" when it comes to electing our representative government. With all the power concentrated with a small nucleus of rich and influential people we are getting uncomfortably close to that small group of people having control of the country. This system of governing is called, "Oligarchy".

Thus, so much money is now required, even at the state and city level, that the outcome of an election could become hostage to the money-to the detriment of the political agenda.

For sure, the monies involved in the election process are staggering. It has been estimated that the 2016 U.S. presidential campaign may cost at least $5 billion, roughly double the $2.6 billion that was spent on the 2012 campaign, according to a reliable report.

The role of "dark money" in distorting the political process is a hotly debated topic these days. Dark money refers to political contributions from nonprofits who don't have to disclose who their donors are or disclose their expenditures.

Three major factors are contributing to keeping the electorate in the dark as the campaign funds flow in. One is the dark money representing two-thirds of the money spent on advertising in the current elections. The second is the surge in campaign spending thanks to the so-called Citizens United. And the third factor is that the Securities and Exchange Commission (SEC) has been prevented from requiring publicly traded companies to disclose their political contributions.

This is indeed scary for someone who believes that his or her vote is important as an indispensable element in the democratic process. This concern also goes to the integrity of the campaign itself. With the onslaught of ads, talking radio heads, Twitter, and email messages, the electorate must feel like the inhabitants of Dresden during the height of the Allied bombardment in the Second World War. Nothing could be heard and the visuals were brief, powerful, and repetitive.

There is no longer an intelligent, in-depth discourse about the contents and merits of the candidate's political agenda. Every sound bite, irrespective of the type of media, is measured in Nano-seconds and contains not a sliver of factual information about the opponent's program. On the other hand, there are absolutely no limits to the quantity of character assassinations flooding the airwaves. The verbal barrage from one camp to the other is propelled with great ferocity, much like grenades being launched, and it's all about the person, not the program.

Like in a conventional war, the one with the most weapons and ammunition wins. During the election campaign, it is the one with the most money for advertisements, smear campaigns, and campaign staff who has the upper hand. And now with the power and speed of the Internet, the reach and coverage that can be achieved/bought is just phenomenal-and often decisive.

Electioneering is now a full-time job. As soon as you have assumed your legislative duties, the new campaign starts. Every minute from now until the next election has to be used to fill the war chest; fundraisers and solicitations are the order of the day.

In addition to expending a Herculean effort on amassing money, the new legislator and already campaigner has to be careful that nothing is said in those intervening four years that might cause any of the electorate to take offense. In some cases, it might be too late already. With the powerful search engines on the web, it appears that anything you have said or written since you started walking can be extracted and used against you. And it will be!

And common for the campaign of smear and misinformation is that the concepts of "truth" and "facts" are missing, gone like the Dodo bird.

Snippets from a persons past used to describe that persons present intellectual and emotional makeup is not only unfair - it is plainly wrong. We all evolve with time and we may change political affiliations, ideology and tastes. So, when a candidate is accused of being insincere measured by some statements made years ago it threatens to jeopardize the very strength of the political process– the ability to learn and adapt.

As an example of how dangerous it can be to say something, now or later, with which the powerful ruling class or special interests disagree, we can again mention the unfortunate incident involving the oldest member of the White House Press Corps. It is worth noting that the following happened in spite of the freedom guaranteed under the First Amendment of the Constitution. The woman in question was a reporter of Lebanese descent and she had been the passionate champion of truth and the enemy of injustice throughout her active life, and as a reporter was always asking the tough questions regarding the White House's conduct and policies.

She was never afraid of stating her opinion, which, of course, ruffled a lot of feathers with the various presidents and their spokespersons. So one day when she dared express her honest opinion with respect to America's policy in the Middle East, more specifically concerning the plight of the Palestinian people, she was summarily "beheaded" by the press and retired from her job.

Although she apologized later for the language she had used, with the explanation that it did not reflect her true, nuanced view on a very complicated situation, her apology was not accepted by the powerful people she had offended.

She had always been relentless and demanding in her search for the truth, which is what a good journalist should be, and she undoubtedly misspoke on many earlier occasions. But what she did not count on this time was that the direct attack on this holy ally would be the straw that broke the camel's back. Although she was just venting her frustration and said something about a topic that most Americans dare not touch, she was immediately condemned by the "word and thought police" and accused of behavior unfitting a reporter. And unlike most politicians who misbehave or misspeak, she was not forgiven.

Here is a very well-respected reporter, ninety years old, who has covered U.S. presidents since Eisenhower and who, in a fit of frustration, utters some strong words about a Middle Eastern policy problem, and she gets the boot right away. The White House Correspondent's Association publicly called her remarks indefensible, her speaker agency dropped her, her book project was terminated, a journalist reward with her named was retired and a planned commencement speech was cancelled. The U.S. president even went so far as to label her comments "Offensive". That was indeed cruel and unjust treatment. So much for guaranteed "Free Speech!"

A more recent example involved the Director of Agriculture, who was summarily fired based on some out-of-context paragraphs from a speech she made years ago. The director, herself an African-American was accused of racism involving a white farming couple. Even though that same couple came to her defense and furthermore lauded her for having helped them save their farm it did not help her regain her job.

These actions defy common sense and it gives the First Amendment of the Constitution a black eye.

This ought to be a warning to especially young people who now grow up in George Orwell's "Big Brother" scenario, where every word they utter and every personal photo taken will last forever and be available to everyone. This gives a whole new meaning to the expression "youthful exuberance," which has been used often to characterize follies and misdemeanors committed in one's younger days. As such, these were usually ascribed to the process of maturing and of feeling one's way in the new world of sensations. Like the shoes and shirts from yonder, they no longer fit and can thus be thrown out.

But now with the unlimited capacity of the World Wide Web, powerful search engines can locate your every utterance and personal photos from the day you started walking on this earth. Employers use this tool to get a better factual impression of the potential new hire, which means that even minor indiscretions and offenses can come back to haunt you-this in spite of the fact that these instant snapshots of your past are usually taken out of context.

Common sense therefore tells you that you should be very careful with what you express in writing and how you appear on photos and in home movies. Whatever is sent to a relative or to a "good" friend can sometimes very easily find its way to the larger forum, that being the rest of the world. This is unfortunately the sad truth when it comes to photos of young girls taken in moments of privacy. A whole net based industry has exploded exploiting these unsuspecting victims to the netherworld of pornography and illicit sex trade. The only common sense advise which can be given to any and all young persons is, that "do not ever send anything by an electronic medium which you do not wish to show to the world".

CHAPTER 8

Price to be paid!

ON DECEMBER 15, 1791, the Bill of Rights (the first ten amendments to the **Constitution**) was adopted, having been ratified by three-fourths of the states. The second Amendment reads as follows:

> *"A well regulated militia, being necessary to the security of a free state, the right of the people to keep and bear arms, shall not be infringed."*

This short sentence, as interpreted by the US Supreme Court (SCOTUS) and seconded by the National Rifle Organization (NRA) has been interpreted to mean that every citizen of the United States of America has the right to own and bear arms – any type of arms. This includes all forms of firearms, from hand guns to automatic rifles.

In spite of the horrific massacres over the last couple of decades involving the slaughter of young and old in schools, theaters, churches and shopping malls, any call to restrict or regulate the availability of guns has fallen on deft ears.

Every time one of these mass shootings takes place the news are followed by hand wringing, communal tears and public announcements by mayors, police chiefs and relatives of the victims. The script is the same and sometimes even the US President steps in and conveys his condolences to the families of the affected.

Questions are asked as to how this could happen and the motive of the perpetrator(s) including their life stories and possible state of minds are being investigated and thrown about by the media for some days or weeks after the shooting – until it happens again - somewhere else. Then the whole process is repeated, only with new victims and different mayors.

If just a fraction of the deaths attributed to guns in the US were caused by any other means these would either be banned outright or at the least be subjected to very rigorous safety measures. Case in point is the attention paid to the dangers caused by unsafe vehicles, drunk driving, airline safety and the efforts to limit unacceptable accidents and deaths by OSHA, FAA, FDA etc.

There is furthermore the danger that with the increased number of dysfunctional, disturbed, and angry members of our society, the firearm becomes the preferred tool resorted to in cases of disagreements and disputes. It becomes an arbiter replacing verbal approaches of solving differences of opinion. This can already be seen as witnessed by the increased gun violence towards abortion clinics and doctors.

It is a rather enigmatic truth that we as a nation will spend billions on fighting international terrorism and absolutely nothing on fighting domestic terrorism.

But since gun ownership is the constitutional cornerstone of American democracy and an inherent birth right, why not treat gun violence as an unavoidable risk and tailor our society accordingly. The common sense approach would therefore include increasing the number of armed guards at all public and private institutions, safety checks at all schools, hospitals, bus stations, theaters, shopping malls and restaurants and in some cases wearing bullet proof garments.

And when mayhem strikes and people are maimed or shot dead, regard it as just another prize one has to pay for the nation's right to bear arms. That way it will become a calculated risk of living in a society which prioritizes the private ownership of guns over public safety. And massacres such as "Virginia Tech" and "Columbine" could be labeled "Collateral Damage".

The present U.S. society is like an old house, which over the years have had additions, revisions and repairs made to it. The original floor plan is almost unchanged, however most of the interior and the utilities have been tinkered with. When something broke, a fix was devised. This was done by repairing the existing or replacing it with something new – always subjected to the existing envelope of the building. Whenever something new was invented, the implementation was always restrained by what had been done before and the space available.

A lot of changes have happened over the last 250 years since the Signing of the Constitution, and we have tried as best we could to shoehorn these changes into the confines of this constitution. Amendments have been added, like extra rooms above the attic and new windows have been inserted in the living room. New updated plumbing has been installed and the kitchen has been remodeled.

But, it's still the same old house.

Maybe we need to sit down and design a new house, a house which accommodates all these changes and which allows for further expansion and modernization. This could be done without sacrificing the good things of the old house. The old fireplace, the sturdy cabinets and the cozy, intimate family room, where generations learned from one another – these could easily be implemented in the new house as a part of the basic design concept.

We have to decide which type of society we want to have. Do we want to have a "Socially responsible and responsive society" or do we want to have a "Darwinist society", where only the strongest survive – and let it be said, the weaker perish?

Maybe a "re-modelling" of the "Constitutional House" is in order? This should be done by qualified craftsmen, architects and engineers, i.e. U.S. Congress. The current method of applying estimators and assessors such as SCOTUS to fix leaks and breakdowns has run its course and it will no longer be sufficient to serve the American people in this new century.

If the dead could speak, gun control would have a lot more votes.

CHAPTER 9

Women's Rights

THE WOMEN IN the U.S. don't know better, but they still think that they are pretty emancipated. The truth be told, they are way behind women in most other industrialized countries in the world. Well, yes, they have the right to work-more and for less-and that's about the only right they have. In most other countries in the world, industrialized or not, women have fundamental rights about their whole productive role, from family planning to assistance during pregnancy and help with child rearing. This is expressed in extended leaves of absence-with pay, before and after birth. The assistance by government extends through the first period of the new life of the child, and it gives the mother the time and means to concentrate on the important first months of motherhood.

Even though most physicians in the U.S. today laud the benefits of breast-feeding, there is almost no time or space set aside for that essential activity in the American workplace.

The U.S. is one of the few countries in the industrialized world that does not have paid maternity leave. The explanation often given for the total absence of any paid maternity leave is that it would have a detrimental effect on the competitiveness of American business, i.e., productive hours would be lost. Well, these costs will also have to be absorbed by companies in other countries, so why is it that American companies cannot do the same without their competitiveness being jeopardized? The speculation is that rather than pointing to the failure to compete they should have said that the earnings per share and the subsequent management bonus would take a hit.

Part of the explanation, of course, is that in other countries, there are a lot more possibilities of getting help from a combination of private and public sources. This covers salary before and after delivery, day rates, and even paternity leave for the father of the child. This last one gives both family members a chance to form a closer bond with the new child during the early, crucial time of the baby's life.

The other part of the explanation lies with the old-fashioned attitude in the U.S. that pregnancy does not belong in the workplace! There is still the attitude that pregnancies are "inconvenient" and somehow disruptive. So one of the most important roles for a woman, that of procreation, is often being treated in the workplace as a disease!

In addition to suffering a setback in pay during maternity leave, the woman often also experiences a blow to her quest for furthering her career within the company. She will feel like a pro baseball player falling behind in spring training, and this phenomenon is often suspected of contributing to the very low number of women in the executive suites and boardrooms across America.

There is currently a push to expand paid maternity leave in the United States. One organization supporting paid maternity leave is Moms Rising. The National Partnership for Women & Families is also an organization that strongly supports paid family and medical leave. But in the interim, it is disheartening to note that the women of this country do not raise their voices in a fit of outrage over this demeaning situation. Again, the richest country in the world cannot-or will not-compensate new mothers for lost income.

The nation's apparent lack of appreciation for the plight of women extends to assistance given to single mothers trying to support and raise their children alone. Whereas single mothers in other countries are offered reduced costs or free day care, in addition to monetary support and child support, the young single mothers of this country are left to fend for themselves. It is often impossible for these women to be able to afford day care. And if not, they cannot hold a job! This onerous plight is often aggravated by the fact that the father of the child feels no obligations toward helping to support his child. And the system in place, if there is such a system, of establishing proper child support payment and enforcing collection is woefully inadequate. This systemic problem across the nation is one of the most important reasons so many of our kids are "left behind." The failure to properly support single mothers at that early time in the child's life will cost the nation dearly later.

In the United States, 21 percent of all children are in poverty, a poverty rate higher than what prevails in virtually all other rich nations.

What is in store for a nation who spends millions on sports arenas

while its children go to bed hungry?

CHAPTER 10

Lessons from Katrina

ALTHOUGH THIS DISASTER happened some years ago, well before this update was written the author has decided to still include it in this tale of common sense. Hopefully what was gleaned from this horrific experience can help prepare us better for next time – and there is always a "next time".

The devastating effects of the natural disaster in the Gulf Coast area caused by the hurricane Katrina were greatly aggravated through human errors, mismanagement, and simple incompetence. The hurricane, which was labeled a category-3 storm by the time it hit New Orleans, had been kept under observation for a week as it worked its way across Florida toward the U.S. Gulf Coast. Very little seems to have been done during that period of time in order to prepare for the impact and resulting calamities. Back-up assistance crews, fresh water, and other emergency planning was not being carried out.

Most of the lives lost were in New Orleans, where the levee system catastrophically failed, in many cases hours after the storm had moved inland. The most property damage, however, took place along the coastal areas at Mississippi's beachfront towns.

The utter lack of preparation, years of neglecting the strengthening of the levees, and failure to properly address the continuing erosion of the marshlands turned an otherwise manageable situation into total mayhem.

Hurricanes are not a new phenomenon in the Gulf Coast. So, common sense should have urged state and local government a long time ago to assume the responsibility of preparing the city for the inevitable event. Strengthening the levees would most certainly have reduced the loss of life and the extent of the property damage. On the Gulf Coast itself, there probably would not have been much that could have been done to reduce the damage. The floating casinos were, of course, no help as they turned into huge wrecking balls. But still, the damage control and post-hurricane assistance could have been better organized.

The United States Coast Guard (USCG), National Hurricane Center (NHC), and National Weather Service (NWS) were widely commended for their actions, accurate forecasts, and abundant lead-time. It was just a pity that this lead-time had not been used for preparation.

Unfortunately the flood also managed to expose the dark underbelly of the American economic success story. TV footage of the looting in New Orleans was continuously being beamed into most American homes. Some of what we saw was undoubtedly a rightful quest for food and fresh water; however, it became quite clear judging from the TV footage that most was "acquisition by opportunity" (looting). This was an unfortunate sign of the lack of civilized behavior (ethics), which sometimes rears its ugly head. We were again uncomfortably reminded of the pervasive poverty in our "third world," which most often does not make it to the evening news.

The hurricane and ensuing flood also exposed the impotence and mismanagement of the Federal Emergency Management Agency (FEMA), which at that time was headed by a presidential-appointed former horse owner. Its incompetence was an embarrassment to the White House and in the later consolidation of government agencies, FEMA was rolled into the new Department of Homeland Security. Let it be said that the head of FEMA was relieved—and so was the Gulf Coast!

Where was the worldwide outpouring of sympathy and donations by countries such as Sweden, Germany, and Spain—and where were the pop stars when we needed them? Where were the collections organized by European jet-setters and records made by well-to-do stars for the poor victims of Katrina?

It has been argued that the reason help from the federal government was so slow in coming to the people stranded in New Orleans was because they were poor, sick, and disenfranchised. There was even the allegation that racism played a role-as if the flood waters knew the difference between rich and poor or black and white! No, the truth here is a lot simpler. Those in charge of the government organization FEMA were simply incompetent and did not plan for the protection of the people.

The fact that so many of those left behind in New Orleans were poor or sick was only due to the fact that they were the ones who could not get out of the city. This was not an example of racism or favoritism, but purely a case of incompetence and mismanagement by well-connected and well-paid public officials. If these officials had had jobs in the private industry, they would not have had a job for long.

And, lo and behold, the mother of incompetence, the head of FEMA, Mr. Brown, was not what he seemed to be. He was hired to be manager of the largest crises-handling and fire-fighting organization in the U.S., and he was not even a manager. He did not have credentials that would even remotely have qualified him for the position. But he had political connections and because he had provided the Bush election campaign with enough funds, he had been bestowed the very important job as head of FEMA. We would all have lived in ignorant bliss about his shortcomings were it not for the fact that he was all of a sudden called upon to demonstrate his curriculum vitae.

I think we should all be very happy that airline pilots and power plant technicians are not appointed through the political crony process!

You could almost call this process of political payback "equal opportunity employment" for politically connected people who cannot otherwise get a job.

Katrina furthermore showed to the world how negligent or incompetent the previous administrations of New Orleans have been. They had not improved the infrastructure and the flood precautions, and they had ignored the low morale of the police force. When Katrina hit, it became clear that they had reaped what they sowed! Only it is always the poor and the sick who have to pay the price and endure the agony. Common sense says that the flood improvements and control management should have been prioritized years ago. When Katrina hit, it was already too late.

CHAPTER 11

And Now, for the Count

WHY IS IT always so important for reporters to mention the number of dead people? Is a catastrophe measured by the number of dead, or by the situation for the survivors? Unless you happen to be one of the deceased or if it is one of your loved ones, is there a difference in the intensity of grief just because the number of dead people increases from 234 to 456? Is it at all relevant to have a number to feel the pain? And can we feel the pain of others? Is the counting of dead people an attempt to increase the feeling of pain and agony-as if two hundred dead is twice as terrible as one hundred?

At the height of the Katrina debacle, reporters were trying to outdo each other by predicting totally unbelievable numbers of perished in the thousands. At least this time we were spared the ridiculous and tremendously offending qualification that is often used when an accident happens in a foreign country. It goes like this: "The Air Ethiopia plane, which crashed shortly after takeoff, killed all of the two hundred and thirty passengers and the ten-person crew on board, but no Americans were among the victims." It is almost as if the incident did not happen when there are no Americans involved. If this is done on purpose or if it is just a way of telling the American public that they do not have to worry and call Air Ethiopia to check passenger lists is not clear. This wording unfortunately has the implicit connotation that American lives are worth more than the lives of people from other nations.

With respect to the real value of mentioning any number larger than ten in a newscast, you could question the impact of that on the listener. There is no doubt that the newscaster seeks to make the event more important by reeling off a lot of high numbers. The truth of the matter, though, is that none of the listeners have any idea how to relate to these numbers. Attempts by the more clever reporters to put these numbers in perspective are laudable, but most likely just as useless.

To illustrate length in a more communicative manner, they will say that the number of cars is so astronomically high that if they were put end to end, they would reach around the world six times. I do not believe that clarifies it to the listener any more than saying that there were many cars. It is, after all, not too important to most listeners to know how many cars there were, only that there were many.

Football stadiums are often used and so is the height of the Empire State Building to depict size and quantity. When we are told that another eighteen thousand soldiers are being dispatched to Afghanistan, we really do not grasp how many that is, as compared to twenty thousand soldiers for instance. The word "thousands" does, however indicate to the listener or reader that it is a large amount. It is therefore more the magnitude rather than the number which makes an impact. Or what about Mr. Bernie Madoff's billions? This love for emphasizing the problem with these large numbers is like a cook adding spices to the food; the only problem is we cannot taste it when too much is added.

Why is it that we spend so much time and effort on the insignificant parts of life? A jury selection in Miami, a fender bender in Atlanta caused by an off duty cop, a kitchen fire in Tulsa, a beauty queen in Reno and on and on. The larger more forward looking challenges to our health as a people and as a nation are casually noted on page 8, if at all. These notable challenges are the education of our children and young adults, the reparation of our decaying infrastructure, future irrigation of large parts of our country, fixing the deficit which threatens to squeeze the prosperity out of future generations, ensuring continued renewal energy while keeping pollution in check and last but not least design and introduce a health care system which is fair and cost effective.

These topics are not topical. They do not help sell the news and thus they are not newsworthy. But they are essential for our survival.

Wake up, and Smell the Roses

THIS TITLE IS, of course, predicated on there still being roses! That might not be so for long, according to many environmentalists who say that if we continue our consumption and waste, there will only be parking lots, pets, and houseplants to remind our children in the future of what was once a world of thriving flora and fauna.

At the international climate change conference in Paris, the general consensus was that something had to be done to reduce the waste and devastation of climate and environments globally. For the first time it seemed as if the seriousness of the situation was recognized by most of the countries participating and ambitious levels of emission and timelines were agreed to.

The nations with larger economies, who are responsible for most of the damage done, seem unwilling to sacrifice their wealth and prosperity with major changes toward behavior commensurate with the size of their global footprints. This is especially true for the U.S. and increasingly also for China, both of whom consume the most raw materials and spew pollutants and toxic effluents at an exponential rate of increase.

The developing countries, on the other hand, are fully concentrating on feeding and housing their populations while at the same time trying to increase their gross national product (GNP). They neither have the luxury of considering the cost of not doing anything or the funds for doing something.

They are first and foremost interested in raising the cost of living of their population. Besides, they know that most of the destruction is caused by the large, industrialized countries, and that's also where the funds are to carry out a deceleration or a reversal of the ever-increasing attack on the world's resources and their resulting effect on a healthy habitat.

We, as a people and as individuals, can truly make a difference in our own ways by reducing the energy consumption and waste in our own daily lives. But to really make a difference, the large, international companies who are currently operating worldwide with impunity and with a voracious appetite for markets and raw materials will have to change their company mission to reflect a greater respect for the balance of nature. This is a bit of a conundrum as these multinationals' single-minded mission is that of generating an ever-growing profitability for their owners or shareholders. Most annual reports today contain a "Green Mission Statement" for the sake of appearing environ-mentally conscientious; however, the reality is that they are probably referring to a different type of "green."

There is also another challenge in our quest to make the world "greener" and more livable, and that is the employment factor. When we strip the rain forests of the Amazon, when we remove mountains in the Borneo jungle and fill their rivers with arsenic to get the gold out, and when we strip-mine large areas of pristine nature, jobs are created and mouths are being fed.

This is extremely important to understand. Without a sustainable em-ployment base, any real accomplishments aimed at saving the rain forest, the polar bear, and the pristine wilderness areas are DOA. You simply cannot stop logging and mining in the name of preservation of the environment if you cannot offer alternate employment as an offset.

Common sense therefore tells us that there are trade-offs that have to be made when we walk toward greener acres. We have to prioritize since the world does not have unlimited funding, and we have to make certain that the changes do not lead to unemployment and devastating displacement of people. More importantly, it is in the long-term interest of every country in the world to make sure that local populations join in the proceeds from the raw materials being extracted from their lands. As it is now, only little or none of the revenue extracted from the forests, the mines, and the wells of particular countries ever finds its way back to the people of that country. The beneficiaries are usually a small cadre of rulers and their accomplices – aided by the multinational prospectors and developers.

This is not sustainable! So, while we are occupied with making the world a greener place, let's also promise to make it a fairer place for all.

CHAPTER 13

Living Backwards?

THE FAMOUS DANISH philosopher, theologian, and psychologist Søren Kierkegaard had a very profound and artful way of describing the conundrums of life, which went something like this: "We should learn life backwards, but live it forwards." Others have said it similarly: "Don't look in the rear view mirror to read the signs for direction when you are going somewhere."

But that's not what we seem to be doing today. We are forgetting the "experience" part and concentrating on the "living forward" part only. We are constantly deferring questions of life and living to the younger people, long before they have gathered any life experiences. What are we to learn from someone who still has most to learn? How are we going to move forward as a species when we apparently have learned nothing from the past?

Today, there is such a focus-almost adulation-toward young people and the culture of youth, to the point where it looks like we have severed the continuity between the ages. There has always been a healthy dose of experimentation and visits into uncharted areas by the young. Sometimes that has resulted in injuries; sometimes it has led to new discoveries and better ways of doing things. But there was always a forward motion, the same way that one gets up higher and higher by using steps on the ladder of life, a ladder which others have build earlier. Today's preoccupation with young people, mostly in the name of profit, is akin to staying at the bottom of the proven, existing ladder while trying to make another one-albeit without having first learned the skills.

American society seems to have reversed life's natural progression-which is: first you are born and innocent, and then you are young, exuberant, learning, and trying to find yourself. After that you get to middle age, where you are working hard using previously earned skills, and, lastly, you enter into old age, which is characterized by arthritis and accumulated knowledge of life.

In earlier days, knowledge, history, and experiences were handed down from society's elders. There was even a connection, a "shortcut," made from the grandparents to the grandchildren, creating a continuum, while the parents were busy toiling in the workplace. This made great sense; a strong family bond was created and society was advancing based on accrued learning.

In the meantime, two things have happened that have broken this historic connection. First, modern families in America have been dispersed all over, and the grandparents no longer live close to their grandchildren. The second one is the development toward a "youth culture," which seemingly does not want any inputs from history or ancient (common) knowledge and experience. The older experienced folks are discarded like used pizza boxes.

It's almost as if young people have formed their own class, not as a political party, but as a powerful consumer and trendsetting force. This is a class that sets its own norms unfettered by humanity's hard-earned respect for history. And their parents have willingly gone along for the ride. They have no choice since they have abdicated their traditional disciplinary roles to the rest of society, to the teachers, sports stars, musicians, friends, and TV – and now to the electronic gadgets. Besides, they are too busy working to feed the youngsters' ever-increasing hunger for entertainment and "things."

This is a worrying trend, especially in a democratic society whose strengths and integrity depend on a knowledgeable, engaged, and informed constituency. If we can, we must avoid repeating our past mistakes; this can only be done if we know of them.

There are unfortunately more and more signs of this development among younger people with lack of respect for authority and for older people. One such incident is described in the "Newspaper" section of this book (see *Seattle Times*, June 16, 2010). We have to somehow get back to basics, where the older, experienced people not only set the standards but also instill the discipline in the younger generation. This is in the young generation's own interest, even though they don't appreciate it at the time.

If we don't reverse the disrespectful mindset and resulting behavior, it will become impossible to maintain a society with rules of order-and law and order.

CHAPTER 14

Limited Control-Use It!

YOU ARE BORN, you live, you die. There is not much you can do about two of these, the beginning and the end, but you can influence the middle part. So stop worrying about the last part and do the middle part in full and with zest.

Somewhere along the way, we lost the belief that each and every one of us is in charge of our own lives. Whenever we have a problem nowadays, it is caused by someone else or something else, and we don't think twice about suing someone or something. This "blame game" has seemingly reached a point where it has replaced personal responsibility. This is an expensive game, though, as the costs of litigation and lawsuits are passed on to products and services...and ultimately to the consumers-us!

We have all heard of the cost of malpractice insurance premiums for medical doctors. The increase of the premium for many doctors has been the straw that broke the camel's back, when they finally had to throw in the towel and close their practice. The amounts typically awarded in personal injury and malpractice cases in the U.S. are so astronomical that they defy logic and common sense. As a consequence, premiums have skyrocketed. In the U.S., the punitive awards driven by the jury arrangement have spiraled beyond the pale with lawyers reaping huge rewards.

We have in place a system that not only reimburses for direct, compensatory damages but also for wrongful conduct, punitive damages. These punitive awards are supposed to send a message in an attempt to dissuade the guilty party from ever repeating said conduct. In personal injury and product liability cases, these punitive awards can be quite substantial. Even though the punitive awards are only successfully awarded in half of the cases filed, these are the ones catching all the headlines. Some of them are unfortunately also quite frivolous and clearly without merits. They are often aimed at extracting large amounts from defendants who can clearly afford to pay. This "deep pocket" strategy is frequently targeted at everyone who has even the remotest connection to the defendant and the case, the theory being that if this "mud" is thrown up on enough walls, it will stick somewhere.

There are, of course, justifications for lawsuits if other ways of settling the dispute cannot be found; however, most often, whenever the "legal sword" is used in the name of serving "Lady Justice," it is not warranted. The legal profession, however, does not object! In most cases, all that is needed is the admission that the culpability is shared in the belief that there are no perfect solutions in this world.

So unless one wants to wait until they get to the "other world," it would probably be a good idea first to see if a negotiated settlement can be arrived at in this world. Again, a settlement, in order for it to be a "settlement," is by nature a two-way street, some give, some take. In this "me world," the "give" part is naturally the sticking point since it is a radical idea that the "me person" could be incriminated or held accountable in any way.

Common sense tells us that for American society to return to a sense of duty and obligation, people have to assume more personal responsibility for what happens in their lives.

"Man is fully responsible for his nature and his choices" (Jean-Paul Sartre)

Many challenges in the world are like walls. We butt our heads against them, and when they don't break or when the headache becomes too excruciating, we give up, sit down, and wait for someone to come by with a jackhammer.

Sometimes you can build a ladder and climb over the wall; in most cases, though, you can find your way around the wall and continue on your way. It is usually up to you to take the initiative; don't wait for someone to help you. The interesting thing is that the more walls you negotiate, the smaller they begin to look.

Degrees of Justice

Below are a couple of real stories that should point to the ridiculous ways in which the sword of justice is being applied. It appears that the punitive awards have no relation to the nature of the accidents and that the mere size of the award is more a testament to how good the lawyer in question is. It certainly has nothing to do with common sense.

——

An elderly man dies from a heart attack while mowing the lawn. The widow sues the manufacturer of the lawnmower for eight million dollars. They settle out of court for two million.

——

In a brutal and senseless robbery attempt, the victim is crippled for life. The assailant gets a five-year prison sentence, but already after eight months for good behavior, he is out again, prowling the streets, ready for another unsuspecting victim. The victims of the robbery—the injured person, his wife, children, close relatives, and friends—all receive no compensation, only grief, pain, despair, and the greatest loss of all: the loss of faith in the American system of justice, itself an unwitting victim.

——

An Oregon jury ordered Ford to pay 1.5 million dollars to the estate of a woman who was killed when a runaway horse she hit crashed through the

roof of her Ford Pinto. Although Ford argued that the case was "one in a million" and no car roof could withstand such an impact, the jury found the automaker liable
(Readers Digest, *May 1986*).

World run amok? So, this teen was wrongfully accused of something he did not do. The case was quickly solved and he did not suffer any harm. These things happen every day all over the world. But this teen wanted to be "made whole" from alleged trauma and damage to his reputation by demanding a payment of $ 15 million from the city and the school, where the incident took place.

Forget it! What about a teenager who loses a soccer game? Should he or she be able to sue the school and the county for damage to reputation and maybe loss of self esteem?

Where are we going with this world if every injustice or personal failure is going to result in a multi-million dollar lawsuit? Someone has to put a stop to this madness. We have to learn from our failures, not profit from them. Common Sense!

CHAPTER 15

Help for the Needy

WE ARE WORLD champions when it comes to collecting money for the victims of catastrophic events, but when it comes to actually channeling that help to those same people in an expeditious and ongoing manner, we are often not quite up to the task

We arrange music festivals, persuade governments to allocate dizzying amounts of funds, and sometimes these funds do get allocated and distributed-at least part of them—in the beginning. But with time comes the inevitable amnesia; the focus turns foggy and finally evaporates into thin air while the world stage turns its attention toward some other calamity somewhere else.

But the worst problem is probably that of execution. When we finally get the money, we do not quite know how we are going to apply it. How do you rebuild life for a man whose existence consisted of selling beach chairs in a tourist spot when the tourists no longer show? How do you build all the destroyed houses in a way that makes them individual and reflects the pride of the owner and the uniqueness of what was?

There are a few organizations around the world who understand how to infuse the money into the local population without poisoning the economic machinery and leading to corruption. But most of the larger organizations are not always capable when it comes to avoiding the side effects of introducing large amounts of money into a fragile and devastated economy without jeopardizing that very same economy.

In order to avoid the damaging effect of corruption at the various levels of distribution, one should work as closely with the final beneficiaries as possible. The purpose should always be that efforts are exerted to have the recipient return to his livelihood, not to make him dependent on the donor. This is often referred to as "help to self-help" and it is priceless, as it reestablishes the pride of self-reliance and industriousness of those people who have suffered the harm and loss of livelihood.

CHAPTER 16

Old Age and Death

WE USED TO say that there are only two sure things in life: death and taxes. We have learned to live with taxes; however, death is another story. You could say that we have not yet learned to live with death. There is, however, another phase that precedes the inevitable. I'm talking about old age.

It is a universal truth that most people want and expect to become old before they finally leave this earth. The wish to get older means aging in a graceful manner, without pain and suffering. Death should not come as a surprise but as a natural extension of life, as it does for most living organisms in the world.

It is a well-known, although less appreciated, fact that old people start out young. It is a less accepted fact, however, that these are both the same person, only separated by time.

So, every person in this world knows that he or she will become old as surely as they will one day die. If you consider this fact, it is very puzzling that so little thought is given while one is younger to the well-being of older people. Since younger people, by extrapolation and given time, will end up being older people, they should make sure that the conditions for older people will be both safe and comfortable.

This means, among other things, that younger people should treat older people with respect in full acknowledgment of and respect for the fact that they have created a world of opportunity for the younger generations. This particularly means that the responsible people-the politicians-should make sure that funds are available for the financing of comfortable retirement packages for the nation's elderly. The "tripod" of senior existence should be supported by the three "legs": housing, adequate food, and medical care wrapped in respect and attention.

Let us not forget: Old age is only temporary.

CHAPTER 17

Focus (Eye on the Ball)

THERE IS ANOTHER thing we must learn to do better if we are ever to solve any of our long-term problems-and let's not forget that most long-term problems stem from shorter-term problems that have accumulated. We have to "keep the eye on the ball." We simply have to focus on the problem for longer than it takes for the newspaper print to dry.

The Katrina debacle opened the eyes of America to poverty and its debilitating effect on the human condition, and there was great indignation sharing the front pages with a call for action. Now, poverty must be eliminated in this great nation of ours. For once we could focus our gaze of benevolence and charity inward, toward our own people. For they were our people, were they not? They lived in America, spoke our language, and shopped in our stores. They were even born in America-but were they our people? Did we feel a kinship with these folks who were clinging to rooftops the same way they were clinging to hope? Or was it only pity and a pang of guilt for some remote members of our race?

We kept our eyes glued to the TV screens and our discussions around the water cooler centered on the government's response-or lack thereof-as well as the fact that the storm had hung out the nation's dirty laundry for all to see.

Now, years later, there is still some minor reporting on the plight of New Orleans and the rebirth of the city as a valuable tourist attraction. A great deal of attention was even paid to Mardi Gras and whether the event should go on as planned. But there are no words anymore of the thousands of homeless inhabitants around the whole Gulf Coast area outside of New Orleans! It is almost as if they have been left to slug it out for themselves—once again out of view of the rest of the American public.

If such a problem as poverty shall ever be tackled, there has to be nationwide attention to the solution, and this attention has to be continuous. Every three months, at least, the leader of the nation and his comrades in Congress should take it upon themselves to "keep the soup stirred" by keeping the people focused on the problem and by informing us of the plans and progress of the program, much like a contractor does with his progress reporting, when he is building a large shopping mall. This has to be done irrespective of the political agenda as it cuts across party lines. It is for the American people of all colors, sexual orientation, and religion.

With the other crisis in the Gulf Coast area, where the oil from a broken BP exploration oil well head contaminated sensitive coastal areas, affecting the lives of birds and animals and the livelihood of workers around the whole region, the president was making an effort to keep the American people updated on a daily basis. But what happens once the well is successfully plugged? The problems were huge and the impact felt for years. But will the American people still get the daily updates?

It is an old truth that whenever there is a catastrophe, the news crew shows up immediately; conversely, when the news crews depart, it is a sign that the catastrophe is over. Not so with poverty, though-it is still there. We need to keep our attention on the solution for the problem, rather than just identifying it.

As the political process today is structured to favor special interest groups, the poor people will often be victims to the transience of our collective memories. We keep forgetting that we suffer from amnesia!

It is a fact that most of the Western world lacks the necessary patience when it comes to staying with a long-term project. This is apparent when it comes to the elimination of worldwide poverty, the protection of our crucially important rain forests, the reparation of our infrastructure, and the improvement of our educational institutions. There is a tendency to live and act in the "here and now." We are so accustomed to having our problems defined and solved within a two-hour span-this being the normal length of a movie. If it goes much beyond the two-hour duration, we start to get antsy and move uncomfortably in our seats. And then we move on.

This is especially true in the U.S., where failure and success are judged daily on the Wall Street ticker. Planning becomes short-term by necessity and true value is many times evaluated using perceptions. This means that it is almost impossible to make plans for long-term objectives, if "long-term" means more than a quarter.

There is a "double whammy" at work here. As mentioned, there is the consideration of stock market forces and subsequent payment of related market performance bonuses, which make a long-term view less desirable for the executives involved. But then there is also the short-time nature of the legislative members' time in office.

The legislator who is in office for only four years is going to be greatly challenged if he has to consider spending his political capital on an infrastructure project that will not be completed until well after his retirement date. So all the cards are stacked against the very projects that are going to secure the proper functioning of society in the future. The future in the U.S., as defined by the business executive, is three months; it's four years as defined by the politician.

Decisions are short-term; solutions are long-term.

CHAPTER 18

The Spirit of the U.S.

HAS THE U.S.A. lost its way? Has the pioneering spirit, which, before, carried generations across the barren stretches of the prairie and through the towering mountains of the Rockies, been extinguished? Or has it just been stowed away, like winter clothes at the start of spring? Or has it been slowly exorcised from our collective minds from too much television and not enough challenges?

This is the country that built the Panama Canal, the interstate highway system and the great National Parks. These accomplishments took a lot of effort, persistence and time. And now we get all worried and angry because we cannot implement a hugely important and intricate health care system in the course of a few months! What has happened to the American spirit?

When you hear the whining, the complaining, and the demanding from all corners of society, old and young, rich and poor, you get the feeling that you are witnessing some sociological test program gone awry.

It's as if a group of writers and comedians have challenged each other to come up with behavioral patterns that could not possibly have evolved through normal evolutionary paths. The test would be to see who could develop the most egotistical individuals and then to throw them together in a society where the only rules are that the ones who end up with the most win.

In this test, you would be allowed to use all means to reach the goal, and you would be allowed to use any interpretation of the rules and laws to your benefit. Common sense should only be used to the extent that it does not constitute an impediment to reaching the goal.

You could say that this is another version of Darwin's theory, in that the survival of the fittest does not lead to a better human but to an animal that is much better at surviving in the hard economic jungles of the new society. The "jungle" has changed, as it has over the millenniums. It is no longer a case of defending oneself against nature's wild animals and the ferocious powers of nature. It is no longer agricultural or industrial survival. No, it is the survival of the individual. And you are no longer using shovels or diesel-driven rock smashers. Today, you use your brain, religion, the color of your skin, your connections, your uniqueness, your lobbyist, and your lawyer. And if that does not work, you remove yourself from the world with sedatives, drugs, and sports. Throughout this, you still demand your rights as an individual. And we are not talking about your right to exist. No, we are talking about your right to get what everybody else has—here and now, and by whatever means.

This "social experiment" has also resulted in some interesting and confusing social mutations. On the one hand, the focus on the individual by design should have led to greater freedom for that individual-to the detriment of everybody else. It did initially, but at the same time there were very powerful interest groups with agendas that attracted these lone individuals and provided them with a group identity, a common cause, and a feeling of purpose. This is very much like what happens when you try to maintain separate droplets of mercury in a bowl; they will inevitably come together as one. Likewise, with the individuals, they will be absorbed by the group and by their persuasions and beliefs.

So, in stead of having a society composed of beings who are independent thinkers with a common-sense approach to life's many variations, we are experiencing more and more of the "group think" phenomenon of larger groups of individuals with the same interests, political or otherwise. These interest groups have managed to make rules and regulations about desired human behavior for that particular group.

The big problem, however, arises when this group starts to impose their world order on individuals not belonging to the group. This innate desire to preach and convert, most often in a militant manner, is becoming a scourge in the U.S. today and it threatens to fracture civil order. In a country as big as America, with its densely populated urban areas, it is essential that people of different "interests" are tolerant of one another. Democracy thrives on different views and benefits from a healthy discourse; it suffers from strife without debates and from Messianic bullying.

An example of this development is the behavior towards smoking. It has been an accepted fact for a long time that smoking is bad for one's health. Smokers are therefore inhaling at their own risk and they would have to pay the ultimate price themselves. Lately, however, with the increased awareness of the dangers of passive smoking, whereby innocent bystanders are inhaling the smoke emitted secondhand, measures have been introduced to isolate smokers from non-smokers.

As everybody is assumed to have the same rights to go to restaurants and to workplaces, rules have been introduced that should satisfy the smoker's rights to smoke and the non-smoker's right to be in a smoke-free atmosphere. Where the division would be impractical, like, for instance, in the workplace, the rule was amended to exclude smoking in such areas. There would still be an allocated place for smokers, whose rights, of course, should also be considered.

There are very few people today who do not seriously believe that smoking is bad for you and that ideally everyone should stop smoking. However, it is still assumed that an individual can do to him- or herself what he or she wants, assuming that it does not hurt anybody else. Under this premise and with the knowledge that smoking is an addiction, it is only fair to accommodate the smokers whenever possible, much like we have introduced measures to accommodate disabled people in many parts of our society. Again, in the case of smoking, we should honor the rights of both parties and introduce measures to isolate smokers from non-smokers.

The operative words here are "rights" and "isolate." However, getting back to the earlier referencing of Messianic bullying, smokers are increasingly being treated as modern-day lepers. The anti-smoking groups have concluded that since smoking is dangerous, it should be banned-everywhere. This "simple" solution would, of course, solve that particular problem; however, if this is the way in which we chose to solve our problems concerning dangers to our citizens, we would probably also have to have a much closer look at our cars, gun laws, consumption of soda, skiing, lawn mowers, and sports activities, just to name a few.

"Banning" seems to be such a convenient tool for controlling behavior, and it is increasingly being favored by politicians who wish to enforce their own beliefs on the masses. The problems are that not only does it increase the criminalization of the country, but it also infringes on the personal rights of the citizens. So instead of living with our differences, and, in the case of smokers, showing tolerance through accommodation, we have decided to marginalize the smokers and subject them to "behavioral terror."

Instead of labeling smokers "lepers," we must accept their addiction and at the same time try to help them cure it. You don't stop smokers from smoking by banning smoking, just as you don't stop teenagers from having sex by telling them to wait.

But this "behavioral terror" is not a new invention. Our kids have experienced it, albeit in its mildest form of parental discipline. As parents, we try to impose our values and society's rules, as we perceive them, on to our children. When they are younger, the operative word is "impose," whereby the rules of their world are the rules we set. This is called "disciplining". As they grow older, we have to let go by starting to treat them as other individuals with their own rights and perceived reality. If the rules of the home do not differ largely from those of society, the transition that the young people will experience will be fairly seamless.

There are numerous examples of behavioral terror (the control of the few over the many) still well and alive in the U.S. These span from prohibiting sexual behavior among consenting adults to eliminating games for kids in order to protect their "psyche," prohibiting use of tanning booths, bans on X-rated book stores or sometimes just of "offensive" reading material, regulations for construction of dog houses, bans on abortion, etc.- all areas where someone's beliefs or religious convictions are imposed on somebody else, usually with the only excuse being that we, the societal "we," are trying to protect the individual. These people are usually oblivious to the fact that nobody asked them to "protect" anyone.

Some of this behavior is often labeled "nanny-ism," the connotation being that complete strangers feel they have not only a right, but also the obligation, to tell you how to live your life. This missionary attitude is leading to a lot of unnecessary friction and is intruding on the privacy of the individual. It also invariably leads to more regulations and rules- written by the few but in the so-called "interest" of the many! These "do-gooders" preach with an almost religious fervor about their duty and right to meddle in other people's affairs.

An example of how much logical thinking has become a victim of this misguided terror is the gun laws in the U.S. Here is definitely an area where a right of an individual can have much more serious effects on other individuals than just that of a bit of cigarette smoke. The logic that guns kill and that any individual should be banned from buying one is still being held hostage to a belief that owning a gun is a birthright and that it is covered by the Second Amendment to the Constitution (from 1789!). So, we are being forced to ban smoking because it kills, but we are not allowed to ban guns, even though they create just as much misery and mayhem as cigarettes do!

Another control lever which is often used to force exceptions to the legislation fabric is religion. This would seem to be in violation of the original intent of the country's forefathers who went to great lengths to separate state from religion. But in a narrow decision by the U.S. Supreme Court the rights otherwise reserved for individuals to oppose the laws of the land for religious reasons was extended to include corporations. In particular certain business owners can reject on religious grounds the 2010 health-care-law's mandate to provide employees with birth control coverage. This allows business owners to weasel out of their legal obligations and stick the rest of us with the bill.

The owners of a chain of stores called "Hobby Lobby" took offense to Obamacare when it was introduced. In particular, they really did not like the part that requires insurance companies to cover contraceptives. Normally, people who don't like a law petition the government to change that law. That's how a nation of laws works.

But these men were Christians. The Supreme Court ruled that Christian business owners are special. Their deeply held religious belief that some particular form of contraception is immoral carries more weight than the force of law, five conservative Christian justices ruled. The court - in a fairly bold admission that its ruling is incoherent - added that no general amnesty from other laws should be assumed to be the result of its ruling and that its reasoning was strictly limited to women's contraception. Such a limitation raises legitimate questions about the rather perverted and obsessive minds of the five men who made the ruling, but it also carries little legal weight. Precedent is precedent, whether the precedent-setters say so or not.

As Justice Ruth Bader Ginsburg wondered aloud in her dissent, "Would the exemption extend to employers with religiously grounded objections to blood transfusions (Jehovah's Witnesses); antidepressants (Scientologists); medications derived from pigs, including anesthesia, intravenous fluids, and pills coated with gelatin (certain Muslims, Jews, and Hindus)?"

There is, however, a much more dangerous beast that rears its ugly head from time to time. That is the threat from the "purists" and the "revision-ists," the first of whom wish to burn books and the second of whom wish to change the contents of books. For the ones who witnessed the book burnings of Hitler's Third Reich, it was absolutely inconceivable that such events could take place in the twenty-first century, or at any time in the future, for that matter.

The basic reasoning of the totalitarian state of Germany at that time was that if you burn the books, you also eliminated the thoughts and views ex-pressed in them. Little did they know of the human capacity for thoughts, which survive in the living.

Rather than destroying the whole book, the revisionists, on the other hand, want to alter its substance. These people are convinced that if they change the content, they will protect the reader from language or subject matter that would be offensive, against which the reader should be shielded. It does not seem to bother these revisionists that in doing so they are commit-ting literary terrorism. They might as well burn the book.

If you get offended by reading the book, don't read it. If you do not like broccoli don't eat it.

Under the freedom guaranteed by the Constitution, these people have every right to their own opinions, and if they find that some reading material is offensive or does not reflect their beliefs, they have every right to refrain from reading it.

Despite the fact that the U.S. prides itself on being the "Land of the Free," it is increasingly being shackled with frequent and onerous regulations and rules. As soon as a problem arises, some action group, politician, or the leg-islative body will propose new rules or amendments to existing rules, which supposedly will help alleviate it.

But since society consists of individuals, millions of them, attempts to control or regulate the behavior of so many, all with their own mind and cultural baggage, can be quite daunting. It will also invariably end up being fair to some and unfair to others. And it can lead to a lot of complexity, so much so that one might require legal assistance to interpret the meaning and the impact of one's actions.

Whoever has tried to park a car in Manhattan, New York, will nod his or her head in agreement. Reading the parking signs is easy enough if they haven't been adorned by graffiti; the type is clear and the font is big enough. But understanding what it says is a whole other matter. The result is usually predictable: that upon returning from a short errand, one finds an official piece of paper secured by the windshield. This is one example of regulation that is well intended but too complicated to understand and to execute. The complexity in formulation defeats its intended purpose; and so it is with many more hastily drafted regulations.

CHAPTER 19

Sex in the U.S.A.

THERE IS AN ambiguity in the U.S. when it comes to sex and sexual conduct, more so than in the rest of the industrialized world. It may not be apparent to the ordinary citizen, but there is a pronounced religious or post-Elizabethan influence in the way sex is being viewed and judged. This goes for everything that relates to the naked body, gays, the sexual conduct of known people, premarital sex, abstinence, and advertisements for Cialis and Viagra.

Sex sells, sex excites, and sex offends.

You can show extreme violence and promote fear; you can even graphically illustrate the plastering of a wall by brain matter from a shotgun blast. But, by God, don't ever let the public get a glimpse of a woman's nipple or the act of a tender, loving sexual encounter.

The sexual drive is one of the strongest in the animal kingdom since it drives procreation and thus the continuation of the species. Different cultures have learned to harness this sexual drive in different ways and have devised customs and standards that help channel it in such a way that it does not threaten the fabric of the local tribe, village, or society.

Let it be said that it is impossible to look at the U.S. as a homogenous society with one set of beliefs, morals, and practices. Because of its sheer size and number of different cultures and religions persuasions, the nation spans the full spectrum of sexual behavior and attitudes. There are also different laws covering sexual behavior for different states, in addition to the federal laws.

There are, however, some overriding traits that separate this nation from most other nations in the world.

(We will not include in this discussion the "wrong side" of sexual behavior, such as deviant behavior, and criminal activity. The topic here is consensual sex among people of a legal age.)

An example of the ambiguity of sex in America is the allegedly taboo subject of the "male member ". Since nudity is often equated with eroticism, the subject of reproductive organs, including the "male member," is a sensitive subject both in schools and in young people's discussions with their parents. In spite of the awkwardness of the subject of sex, the drugs originally aimed at curing sexual dysfunction in men, Viagra, Cialis, and Levitra, are being promoted vigorously and openly on all the networks. As the purpose of these pills is somewhat taboo, the sales message is wrapped in a palatable package of love, walks on the beach, and candlelight. However, the ad, which is being transmitted to everyone, including kids and teens, comes with the following warning: "If the erection lasts for more than four hours, you should consult your physician." So much for being prudish!

There is yet another trait that characterizes the U.S. when it comes to sex, and that is the co-mingling of sexual behavior with celebrities and elected officials. It seems to appear as somewhat of a surprise to most when they find out that the people they have appointed, respected, and admired also have a sex life.

As a case in point, probably one of the more widely reported cases involved a former president who enjoyed a well-publicized sexual encounter in the White House. Well, we don't know for sure, but we are assuming that he enjoyed the act as much as anyone else would! We should not have been shocked that such a charismatic person in the most powerful position in the world had a sex life, but the problem in this case was that he was married.

His infidelity should have been a matter between him and his wife, and should have been of no concern to the nation. It is correct that the act took place at his place of work, but it probably did not influence his work or his judgment before or after. It was therefore not relevant to his position as president. Nor should this have been handled as a sexual activity, but as an act of infidelity. The truth of the matter, though, is that sex titillates; infidelity does not.

What was relevant was the fact that he lied about the incident. While facing the whole nation, he lied with glaring honesty about having "had sex with that woman." This lie was shocking to the whole country and it unfortunately revealed an ethical flaw for which he could have been impeached.

Another publicized case in which sex was co-mingled with a public person involved the governor of New York. After admitting that he had frequented a prostitution ring, starting back when he was still the attorney general, he was threatened with impeachment, but finally agreed to step down. The reason for the outrage and the loss of position here again was not the sex, but the fact that the governor had used as a political foundation the promise that "ethics and integrity" would be an integral part of his administration. He had also preached family values and in his career had prosecuted several prostitution rings in the city. Thus, women's rights groups and anti-human trafficking groups felt that he had betrayed them. So, he was felled not because of the sexual actions, but because of the dishonesty and betrayal. Again it was the sex that covered the news.

In the U.S., there is a tendency to judge an individual's worth and integrity as a person and as a professional on his or her sexual behavior, even when that behavior is quite normal and consensual. Nowhere is that clearer than when the talk turns toward the "gay issue." Many Americans have a hard time accepting that there are people who are attracted to their own sex. They will accept the idea that variants and permutations in other species in the world are normal, but somehow they do not accept this when it comes to human sexuality. They often confuse the two words "norm" and "normal," where the "norm" is that more than 90 percent are heterosexual. That, however, means that the remainder being gay is a "normal" occurrence in terms of nature's permutations. Gays have been accused of suffering from some kind of psychological abnormality and there is often the argument made that, with some help, they could be "cured."

Why this propensity for marginalization of people based on their sexuality? Does it stem from homophobia or is it simply based on ignorance? As a nation, we are supposed to be tolerant and accept people of different color, religion, and sexuality. After all, the important thing is to love—the "who" is irrelevant.

With the current dispute over transgendered persons access to bathroom of their "new" sexual identity in some states in the U.S. the prudish Victorian monster has again reared its ugly head. In some states laws have been passed which bars these transgendered persons from entering the bathrooms of their new gender. The reasoning is that barring the law, men who are now "women" would have access to little American girls in the bathrooms and that this could lead to sexual transgressions, improper touching and possibly rape. This excuse is exceptionally lame and does not hold water. There is absolutely nothing currently which makes it impossible for men to molest and rape little boys in the restroom areas. So what is the difference? Why are laws made that do not have any material effect other than to satisfy some imaginary fears of sexual scenarios by some religious groups who are terrified of different sexual orientations. We already have laws that bar adults from having intimate relations with children – what more is required, other than maybe more education on the topic?

Common sense tells us that America has to adopt a more open and honest approach to addressing sex and sexual behavior at all levels of society. There has to be more efforts made to couple sexuality and responsibility. Especially in today's world, young people have to be told that emotional sex is preferred over casual sex and that at no time should they use sex as an expression of power. It does not make sense to preach "abstinence" to young people with bodies oozing with hormones, but it is essential that they see sex as normal and that they learn to control these sexual drives as they move toward adulthood. Only then will they be able to become responsible for their life and their actions. And we have to teach the young people that there is nothing wrong with the naked human body and that nudity is not the same as sexuality, unless and until it is made so. The problem is that most public relations firms and ad agencies are using the naked or partly naked body as a sexual stimulus to arouse the customers and get their attention.

In the future, it will be even more important that sex is being talked about in America as a normal human drive, one that can be discussed openly. We should all have learned from the terrible silence that enveloped and stifled us during the onset of the AIDS epidemic how important it is to be able to eradicate our collective stigmas (in that case, against gay people). A whole generation of bright and innocent people became the victims of an unnecessary silence just because they happened to be of a different sexual orientation.

Nowadays, we know a lot more about the illness, which was originally referred to as the "gays' disease," and we also know that it still spreads primarily as a sexually transmitted disease, closely followed by "tainted" blood from needles and transfusions. There are virtually whole countries in Africa where AIDS rages with impunity as a result of a refusal to admit that it is sexually transmitted-the denial being a consequence of ingrained cultural norms.

We are being-and will also in the future be-faced with different sexually transmitted diseases of various yet unknown strain, and it will therefore be crucial that we can discuss these topics openly and honestly.

This will require that we treat the subject with care and the people with respect.

CHAPTER 20

Have They Won?

WHEN YOU ANALYZE the situation today in the U.S. and compare it to pre-9/11 times, it appears on the surface that the terrorists with their kamikaze attacks have won a major long-term victory. They have managed to redefine the concept of a "free society."

The freedom to move, to speak, and to work is largely untouched; however, some restrictions have been introduced as a direct result of these unprecedented attacks on U.S. soil. Anti-terrorism measures were signed by executive order by President George W. Bush right after the attack. A number of amendments were added later, among them the Patriot Act in 2006, with the incorporation also of the Financial Anti-Terrorism Act, the aim of which was to interrupt funds flowing to potential terrorist cells.

As a direct consequence of these measures, regular proceedings were superseded or simply overruled, and the rule of law became victim to interpretation—the government's rendition. The critics, and there are many, allege that this anti-terrorism legislation endangers democracy by creating an "acceptable" exception to the normal rule of law and that it allows an authoritarian style of government. The government's response has been that these measures are necessary temporarily to avoid future acts of terrorism.

The key word here is "temporarily." If "temporarily" refers to the time during which terror acts are still a threat to the U.S., then it would be more correct to say, "in perpetuity." Certainly preventive detentions and warrant less searches are here to stay, as are secret wire taps and other forms of subversive "preventive" steps.

Of course, with the ingenuity of future suicide bombers, forever finding new hiding places on or in the body, the regulations for screening at airports will not abate. On the contrary, it will not be long before full-body scans or cavity searches will be the norm of the day—despite the protests of the American Civil Liberties Union (ACLU).

Civil liberties as protected by the U.S. Constitution can be simply defined as an individual's legal and constitutional protection against the government, so any action by the government can, of course, be termed a violation of that protection. The problem is that the ACLU will often selectively decide to invoke this protection where it is often not warranted. The letter of the law says that the individual citizen enjoys protection against the government; however, the spirit of the law says that the action by the government shall be material and it shall in no way prevent the government in its duties to the American society.

So, in the case of rules for air travel screening, the overriding concern for all the passengers' safety and security supersedes the individual's right to privacy protection. Should the passenger feel so strongly about his or her wish to shield the body, that passenger should take the train.

The ACLU concern is probably the easiest to solve. A much greater issue has to do with the actual screening and its effectiveness. One gets the feeling, at least in the U.S., that many of the employees working at the checkpoint and at the X-ray screens are there because it's a paid job, not because they are on a mission. Spot checks have unfortunately revealed that if you are a determined terrorist, there are ways to circumvent the safety checks. A total body scan seems to be the only fail-safe solution.

The situation at the U.S. airports have now gotten to the point where traveling is severely hampered by the check-in procedure. Recently in O'Hare Airport in Chicago lines of over 3 hours processing times developed and hundreds of passengers missed their flights. There is no doubt that unless the process is streamlined and more people are employed by the airport the situation will become untenable. Air travel will suffer greatly.

Granted, a free and open society is by its nature extremely vulnerable to attacks, both from the outside and the inside. Whoever wishes to do harm can select the time and the place. The challenge is to take all possible steps to restrict the means for financing, collection of necessary materials, planning, and execution of any kind of terrorist action. This has to be done at the same time that people's right to privacy has to be honored, and at the same time that people's freedom to move freely throughout the nation is maintained. This is as difficult as texting while driving.

Common sense says that this is akin to two freight trains driving toward one another on the same track. It cannot be done! We have to have two tracks, one that accepts government's wider powers for surveillance under the strict oversight of Congress, and one that ensures that the private information of the individual is kept that way—*private*.

The future threats are not limited to explosives but will most likely also include chemical and biological weapons, the aim being the destabilization of the nation and the destruction of our liberty and the American way of life as we know it. The terrorists have no political agenda; they probably could not even organize a town hall meeting. No, they are only interested in destruction in the name of some deity and for a cause that lies somewhere between hatred and divine obligation.

In order to properly address this threat to our nation and to our system, we have to realize that the war against terrorism has to be conducted on two fronts. We have to take the immediate steps to restrict their access and means of carrying out their evil undertakings. This is very much a defensive tactic against a moving target, and it's much like a blindfolded boxer landing a blow now and then. We are doing this now, and we have to continue and hone our tools in that fight.

On the other hand, we also have to go on the offensive and decrease the terror threat through a long-term policy of marginalizing the hardcore cells through deprivation of members and funds. This is by nature a global effort and it will entail destroying training grounds, sources of income, and the free flow of financial means. This is much like targeting and killing the malignant cancer cells in a person's body by any means possible-chemotherapy, radiation, surgery, or immunotherapy-before the destructive cells spread.

The ideal solution would, of course, be to remove the terrorists' reason for being: poverty and no hope of a future. However, as the world seems to develop in the opposite direction, that of greater division and wider distance between the "haves" and the "have-nots," to wish for a change of that nature could rightfully be labeled "naïve."

We most likely have to accept that we have to live with the terror threat, along with increased surveillance by our government. We should, however, still exercise our freedom by showing that we are not afraid— and then go about our business as usual. That way the terrorists will not have won!

In addition to the increasing but still moderate danger to the nation from homegrown terrorists, we have a much greater and present danger threatening the country from within. This is the cancer of drugs. These drugs which are flowing freely into our country, together with the homegrown variety, could very well enslave large parts of our society while threatening us all with the subsequent scourge of crime in the form of theft, robbery, and bodily harm-crime driven by addiction.

The Victims

This insidious threat to the civil order of our great nation is based on growing addiction, a spiraling demand and an enormous amounts of illicit revenue generated at all levels of the supply chain. In one of our neighboring countries, Mexico, the drug cartels are threatening to unseat the governments in many of the provinces, not by free elections but by the "power of lead," and nobody knows where this could end. The escalating level of corruption is no longer mainly driven by greed but by fear and survival instincts.

With a very productive and ruthless neighbor of drug cartels and a seemingly infinite amount of customers in the U.S., a cocktail has been brewed that can be hard to swallow. As the drugs are the means, and the money the objective, common sense says that the most effective way of conducting this war would be to attack the jugular vein of the money stream.

We have to be much more diligent in barring the drugs from entering this country in the first place. If we can stop Americans from bringing fruits and fresh meat through customs when returning from overseas trips, we should also be able to stop huge amounts of drugs from being smuggled in. This also goes for mass caches of guns and boxes of money being smuggled the other way out of the country.

There's also a more insidious way in which drug dependency has been created; through the use of opiates used against pain. There is greater awareness now, but until recently opiates in the form of pain medication such ax Oxycodone aka Roxicodone and OxyContin were widely distributed my the medical profession. The availability of these prescribed drugs has been reduced – but not the dependency. This of course means that more and more people are resorting to street drugs which carries with it both stigma and exposure to crime. Solving the problem of a "drugged America" is a huge national challenge, especially since the pharmaceutical companies have already acclimated the people to believing, that all and every problem can be solved with drugs.

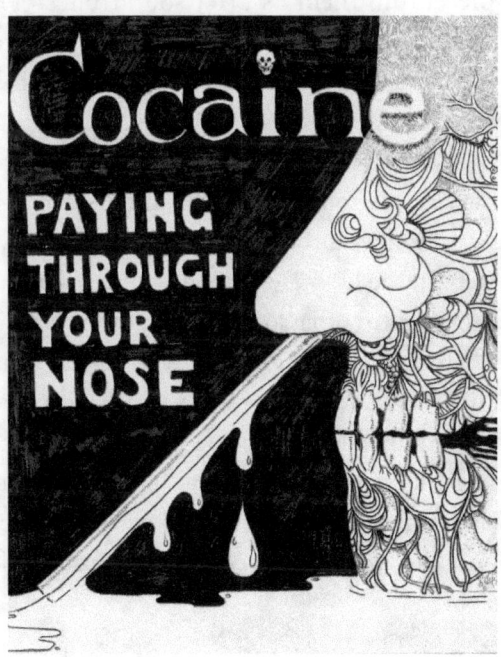

CHAPTER 21

Hero of the Day

THERE WERE JOHN WAYNE, Superman, Charles Bronson, and Schwarzenegger: icons of Hollywood and heroes to the American people. They fit the unwritten specification of killing all the bad guys and doing it within the allotted time, two hours-this being the length of the movie. Of course, there was not supposed to be any visible blood or pain.

This fixation by people on heroes and quick solutions to complex problems carries over to many aspects of everyday life. This is usually abetted by the media's propensity for painting events in the world as one-dimensional by presenting them as brief sound bites. These sound bites usually lack the in-depth explanation and analysis that could expand the dimension and understanding. And that lack of depth can make them extremely dangerous.

A case in point was the sound bite by a former would-be vice president from Alaska in connection with the discussion of a major revision to the present health care system in the U.S. One of the provisions in the proposal by the Democratic legislators was to offer some assistance for old people in assessing their health and financial options to help them decide what to do towards their last years. This was done because it was realized that many of the nation's seniors were ill equipped to evaluate the sometimes-convoluted options and financial arrangements offered to them. This "assistance to the seniors" was conveniently misconstrued by said former would-be vice president in an inflammatory sound bite, which accused the government of wanting to "kill off Grandma."

As a stand-alone message, it was very powerful, albeit totally misleading; however, it managed to rally a great number of anti-government groups, who fabricated their own follow-up sound bites such as: "genocide," "cleansing," and the killing of our old mothers and fathers. That anyone bought this was in itself amazing and very disturbing. It made it abundantly clear how words out of context can damage perceptions, ideas, and relationships. Is it then so surprising that Adolf Hitler moved the masses in the '30s? He was even helped by an almost complete control of the airwaves.

Generally Americans, like most other people, want their life to be simple and predictable, with the universal belief that everything will work out. In today's chaotic world, they try to hang on to some fixed points, like a flood victim hanging on to a tree in the raging stream. They do not have the time or inclination to read beyond the headlines on the front page, with the result that they will make up their minds with their hearts. Passion over prudence.

This desire to have a central figure in their life, someone like a savior, who can solve their problems, leads them many times to direct their attention to the leader of the land, the president. In no other country in the world, outside of indigenous tribes in remote places, is one person expected to carry out so many tasks and to be responsible for so many events as the American president. "The buck stops here" does not mean the Senate or the White House; it means the Oval Office.

These expectations are unrealistic, as common sense would dictate, and the president has to remain cognizant of the fact that even he cannot be everywhere and solve all the problems.

A case in point was the recent catastrophe in the Gulf of Mexico, where the explosion of an exploratory oil platform led to the worst oil spill in the nation's history. Almost from day one, the president was accused of not being in charge and of not being tough enough on the companies having caused the spill. This was a typical reaction by people who wanted someone to blame.

As for the first point of not being in charge, the president could document that he was indeed briefed every day and that his direct subordinate in charge was the commandant of the U.S. Coast Guard. As for the second point, people did not appreciate the truth that there was very little he could do personally to fix the actual spill; he could put the pressure on the responsible culprits, and he did.

Many people urged the president to let the government take over the responsibility of the containment and cleanup. Little did they understand that the government does not have in its arsenal the capability to handle oil well control. That was left to the private sector. Of course, there was the huge problem looming of responsibility, damages, and maybe even criminal charges. If the government stepped in, it would have automatically assumed parts of that responsibility.

In comparison, there was very little the then-president could have done to assist in the safe return of Apollo 13. That had to be left to the professionals. And so it was with the oil spill in the Gulf of Mexico.

Again, the media in its frenzied efforts to inform people of every step of the process omitted to include the appreciation of the technical intricacies of this event. The fact alone that one of the largest oil companies in the world, with all its experienced engineers, consultants, and access to universities, could not solve the problem right away should have given an indication that this was indeed a difficult issue to tackle.

There is no doubt that this incident was a terrible calamity, both for the habitats of the coastline affected as well as for all the people whose livelihood was destroyed. The anger directed at the companies having caused this calamity was understandable. That some of this anger was directed at the president was unfortunate and probably came from the fact, as mentioned earlier, that "the buck stops there."

Common Sense for Humans

These man-made calamities will happen. Not all jobs are totally safe. In our quest for providing the necessary fuel for factories, homes, and cars, we engage in deep shaft mining, offshore oil exploration, and land-based drilling in sensitive areas. It behooves us to take the proper precautions and apply fail-safe methods to the best of our ability. Proper controls have to be put in place and frequent monitoring and checks have to be carried out. Even more importantly, a proper risk assessment analysis has to be carried out and a plan "B" developed. That does not, however, mean that it is risk-free.

It is up to the media to provide the citizens with a balanced view of the risks and benefits of these endeavors. Failure to do so will lead to a lot of misconceptions and, worse, anger. In the aftermath of the oil spill in the Gulf of Mexico, one senator said that by 2020, the internal combustion engine would be obsolete! His knowledge of the world we live in must have some glaring holes. First, the diesel engine is the most efficient heat engine by far in the world, and does he realize that the whole world fleet is operated using internal combustion engines? The message that the media needs to get out to the nation is that we have to apply all forms of energy generators, and only slowly over time can we favor some over others. It is a well known fact though that the fossil based fuels and minerals are finite entities, so time becomes an important parameter. However, one must not forget that there is only so much money in the world for the development of alternate energy generation. Thus, this development has to be guided by facts, economy, and common sense.

The tasks and responsibilities of a modern U.S. president are unreal and humanly impossible. He is seldom praised but he is most often criticized for what he has done and what he has not done. He is constantly being barraged by news pundits, experts, and talk show hosts, who are debating, endlessly it seems, his every word and the ones he hasn't said yet or should have said. This situation is aggravated by the instantaneous dissemination of news, rumors, blogs, Tweets, and news channels 24/7.

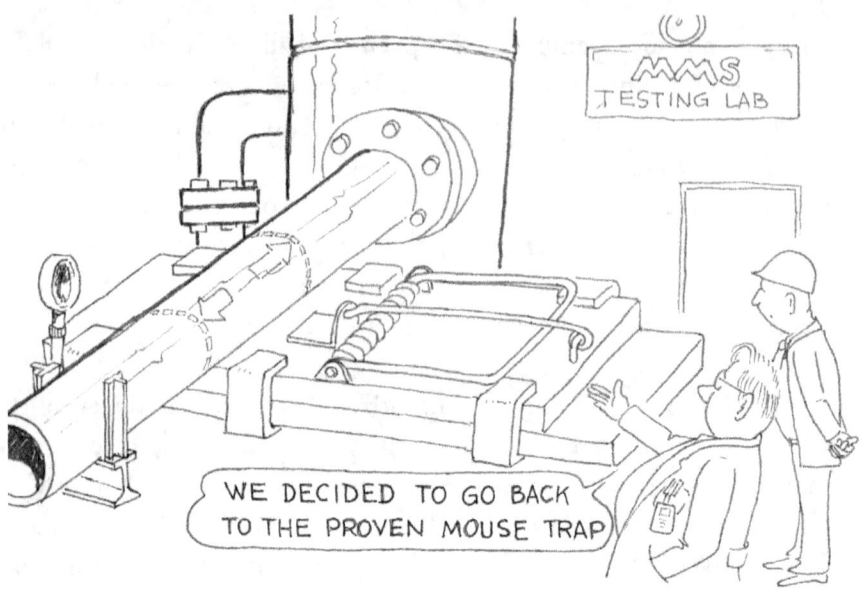

An example of this is an incident during the height of the Gulf Oil spill catastrophe, when the president had assembled the press for an impromptu conference, at which the reporters were invited to ask questions. The same day, the chief executive of the MMS (Minerals Management Service) had left her job. When asked about whether she had resigned or had been relieved of her duties, the president answered that he had not been informed about that yet. The press pounced on that as a sign that the president did not have a clue as to what went on in his administration. This was a distraction from the main issue at hand, namely the plugging of the oil well and the removal of the oil, and it should not have been an issue.

The departure of the head of the MMS was no big deal in the overall context; however, the talking heads made it so. They even went so far as to question the president's leadership qualities. This kind of constant attack is very corrosive and robs the president of time and authority for the most important tasks at hand. And it sends the wrong message to the citizens.

The president is spending so much time defending his actions that he almost becomes paralyzed. The presidency in the U.S. is no longer the office; it's the person. Americans have made it so in their deeply felt longing to have a father figure, a hero, someone who will take care of all of their problems. And they also want to have a scapegoat, someone they can blame as they wash their own hands of any responsibility and ownership.

If democracy is to survive in America, it has to start with the acceptance that an elected official has gotten the job because he or she was elected. This again means that the majority of voters voted for him or her. That is how democracy works. It entails that the people who did not win (this time) have to accept the fact and work with that elected official to the best of their ability for the common good of their constituents. If the "non-winners" of the election turn into obstructionists and nay-sayers, democracy will become the victim.

Unfortunately it appears that the art of compromise and cooperation is disappearing from public discourse. The Balkanization of the nation with the promotion of fractured and dispersed interest groups is winning the day. The result is that even the most mundane issues at hand cannot be brought up for discussion. We have the "Blues" and the "Reds" and there does not seem to be any colors in between. Where are the realists? Where are the grown-ups, the ones who have experienced life in all its facets, who know that life is not black and white? We need some adults in Congress, people who are not beholden to any interest groups, people who have a strong sense of duty and the ethical makeup to show courage and perseverance in the pursuit of solving the nations challenges.

CHAPTER 22

The Pharmaceutical Powerhouse

Americans are consumed by prescription drugs—or is it the other way around?

WHEN THE PHARMACEUTICAL companies were first allowed to advertise their drugs on TV in the U.S., they became the largest drug pushers in the nation. Most of these are prescription drugs. What, then, is the value of pushing/marketing a drug when in the end it will be the physician who writes the prescription, which includes making the choice as to the type, dosage, and brand? Do these companies count on TV viewers pressuring their doctors to choose a special brand, much like they would select a bottle of red wine? At whom are these ads aimed? Could it be that by reminding the public of what is available for various ailments, they will be more aware of symptoms they would not otherwise have been concerned about?

For serious illnesses, the patients will probably not be able to make use of their new found knowledge gleaned from watching television. In those instances, the doctor will prescribe what he thinks is the best cure for the ailment.

Then there are the problems that are not directly life-threatening, but which fall into the category of daily life being full of minor pains and discomfort. Also, here is it prudent for the patient to listen to the advice of the doctor. Evaluating the compatibility and effectiveness of a drug being "sold" on TV is like listening to different companies all selling the best and most comfortable mattress in the world, the one very crucial difference being that the wrong drug could have a much more detrimental effect on your health than a bad mattress could.

Judging from the frequency of the TV ads and the length of each plug (some are lasting over 5 minutes), the pharmaceutical companies must be spending more money on advertisements than on basic research, especially when one considers that a company enjoys seven years of patent protection for any brand drug, which means that the development costs are amortized over seven years.

Drugs today do not only serve a medical purpose; they are increasingly marketed as "wellness drugs." If you suffer from any unpleasant effects of living, there is a remedy that will help you manage the bumps on life's road to happiness. If you ache, if you can't sleep, or if you shouldn't sleep, there's a pill. If you are depressed, there's a pill. If you can't digest the hamburger and fries, there's a pill.

If it's not a car add it's a pharmaceutical add. The car adds tells you that you can drive fast and be successful with women and still keep a perfect hair-do. The pharmaceutical add promises that you can keep this up for a very long time. If it lasts for four hours or more though, you should contact your doctor.

These are know as "Carmercials" and "Pharmercials"

It's almost as if we have divorced our bodies and minds from the laws of nature. Maybe we have traveled too far on the road to a trouble-free existence. If we don't allow ourselves to feel pain, to be tired, to be depressed and moody, and to be naturally joyful, we have lost the ability as humans to control our own existence. We do not get stronger or wiser, only more dependent as we abdicate our responsibility over our own lives while adopting a life of chemical dependency.

Unfortunately we have to a very large extent conditioned our children to enjoy the wellness but not the necessity of labor. We have tried to protect them against disappointments, pain, hard work, and boredom-and what have we reaped? Individuals who collapse at the first sign of challenge and who have to be constantly entertained and amused. There has also been a rash of ADD and ADHD cases fueling the drug development for kids. In stead of solving the underlying problems leading to these behavioral anomalies, such as high sugar intake, lack of exercise and constant stimuli, the kids are only being treated for the symptoms with pharmaceuticals. This development creates a huge opportunity for the drug companies who can thus create a shortcut to a happy life-just by popping a few pills! This is in line with the desire for "instant gratification."

There is some underlying suspicion that the drug companies are not all that unhappy with having more sick and unhappy people than healthy and happy individuals. Profits driven by misery!

Talking about profits, they are huge! In the U.S., with its monopolized health care service sector, there is very little or no competitive pressure to bear on the price of drugs, with the inevitable result that the costs are sky-high when compared with other industrialized countries.

As a case in point, a three-month supply of prostate pills was quoted by the pharmacy at four hundred and twenty dollars; however, when the pharmacist realized that the client did not have health care coverage, the price was lowered to sixty-six dollars. So, is one to deduce from this that the health care insurance provider is billed the four hundred and twenty dollars by the pharmacy? It is no wonder that insurance premiums have skyrocketed.

There is also another new method used to "front-load" the huge billing machine. During surgeries outside help is contracted and machinery and instruments are included on the billing even those might not have been used. Unexpected fees are routinely generated outside the operating room as well.

On the wards, a dermatologist may be called in to examine a rash and perform an expensive biopsy. The person in scrubs who walks a patient to a bathroom for the first time after hip surgery may turn out to be a physical therapist billing $400. Common for most of those fees is that the patient is unaware. He has not been told of those charges up front or those charges are incurred whilst he has been sedated. These huge costs result in pushing the premiums upwards as the insurance carriers are kept whole.

This is exactly what has been missing from the whole health care debate: the costs. The people who are covered by insurance are blissfully ignorant about the actual cost; they only see what they have to pay for the drug at the pharmacy. And if they enjoy coverage through their employer, they have no awareness of the horrendous annual rise of the premiums.

The original concept of an insurance company is that all its members pay into a pool and when someone needs to be healed, funds are paid out from this pool to cover the cost. So, in effect, it does not need to be making money; it just has to have sufficient funds in the "kitty." This is called a "mutual insurance arrangement." The administration of the kitty would be covered from the fund, but there need not be "profit" allocated. This system works as a cooperative, the purpose of which is to spread the risk. In the recent health care debate, this simple concept was accused of being a stepchild of socialism and even communism by the opponents of U.S. health care reform.

Well, if these opponents were concerned about the effects of spreading the risk, why were they not concerned about the huge profits of the health care insurance companies? These companies not only allocate the risk in the form of very high premiums to the policy holders, but they also maximize their own profit by sifting off a large part of those premiums, and by limiting the operating costs through a selective determination of health care coverage for the policy holders.

So, these so-called health care providers reap enormous profits, which go to administration and huge salaries. This is money that should go to health care, but the sad truth is that a bureaucratic firewall has been set up to limit the actual health care being provided to many needy members. There are disturbing tales of the efforts being exerted by the insurance companies to deny rightful coverage to people who have paid their premiums for decades.

Why do people in the U.S. accept this? Probably because they have grown accustomed to the situation, much like sitting in traffic for hours on the way to work every day. They simply have no idea that there are other ways of providing health care to the nation. When someone has tried to inform them of the benefits of nationalized health care systems in countries like Canada, England, and Denmark, the voices of the status quo, the pharmaceutical companies, and, of course, the insurance companies have tried to scare the public with allegedly "true" horror stories.

It is amazing that anyone can be AGAINST healthcare for everyone. There are millions who currently do not have healthcare, i.e. access to health care. Then there are the millions who are covered through their employer. They see that the premiums rise every year, deductibles go up and when they loose the job, they also loose their health care coverage. And the smaller employers can no longer afford the premiums and still stay in business.

So, we all run the risk of being priced out of health care. Right now we have so called health care providers/insurers as expensive gate keepers to how, who and where long term premium payers can get their care. And for that they charge an astronomical fee. On top of that all the different insurance companies each has their own rules and forms to be filled out, which means an undue burden on each and every doctor's office.

It's simple economics 101, that when you have a single payer system and you do not have to pay the insurance companies (health care providers?) and you have a uniform claims system that you are going to save billions.

The richest industrialized nation on earth, the United States of America is the only country who is still not providing health care to all of their citizens. That is going to be catastrophic for the future.

We have indeed as a nation "welcomed the tired, the poor, the huddled masses….", but as a civilized society we have failed to take care of them. One of the more important obligations of a democratic society is ensuring that there is a safety net strong enough to guarantee that the weak, the sick and the poor are helped and taken care of.

A society, which fails to do so is a very poor country - irrespective of its worldly wealth.

One of the often-used questions by the opponents of a government-run health care system is whether people would tolerate having a government layer between the patient and the professional provider. The service would, as they claim, most likely suffer, and, by the way, "We Americans do not ascribe to socialism and communism!" This debate became totally unhinged from facts and reality, especially in light of the fact that few people realized that we already enjoy government-administered services, such as police, Medicare and Medicaid, FAA, etc.

Would we rather have a layer of profit-takers and service-limiters between us and the doctor instead of a layer of government services, even considering that the latter would be far cheaper overall because of its magnitude of scale? Apparently, yes, judging from the debate in Congress and on the airwaves.

If the members of Congress had to purchase their own health care insurance for themselves and their families on the "free" market, with all the limitations to preexisting conditions and occasional refusal of coverage, would this have changed the outcome of the health care debate? You bet it would.

What has been so hard to understand is that so many normal citizens have been adamantly against any changes to the current system. These citizens are either covered, in which case they apparently accept that their premiums go up with double-digit percentages every year, or they are covered but still silently accept that they cannot get the services they need. Or they have no coverage at all.

Common for all the ones covered is the fact that they have to navigate the convoluted instructions on how to figure out co-payments, deductibles, exceptions, length of coverage, and types of available services. And the paper mill is totally different for each company, which puts an enormous burden in terms of personnel and cost on the health care provider, the doctor, and the hospital!

So, why did so many people not want a new, cheaper, and simpler system? Maybe common sense was trumped by influential money!

The dysfunctional health care system with its sky-high prices for drugs has been fueling a parallel market, which could have untold, life-threatening effects on unsuspecting patients. We are talking about the purchasing of drugs from other places than your local pharmacy. This can be mail order pharmaceuticals from out of country (mostly Canada), and drugs bought while traveling overseas (mostly Mexico).

Although people save substantial costs by buying from places not certified, they run a very high risk of getting drugs that either do not work, i.e., are placebos, or work in ways that were not intended, i.e., like poison. Admittedly there are a great number of people in the U.S. who cannot afford the medication they need to stay alive, and for them it's not an option *not* to purchase drugs from unauthorized sources. It's either dying for lack of medicine or dying from taking the wrong medicine. But at least in the latter case, there is the chance that they get the right medicine. It is indeed tragic that citizens in the richest country in the world have to gamble with their health and lives in such a way.

So, again, why are people not more incensed about the status quo? During the health care debate, there was a plethora of stories told by patients and health care professionals, many revealing in gripping agony how sick members of the family were denied coverage only to suffer a painful and premature death. In any other country, they would most likely still be walking among us today. There were stories of how the insurance companies had whole departments whose sole objective it was to find ways of denying coverage to otherwise qualified applicants. This was done to save money, improve the bottom line, and make it possible for executives to award themselves huge year-end bonuses.

Why do most Americans believe that this system is working? And why do so many intelligent and otherwise reasonable people not see that this system is woefully flawed and that their premiums are being siphoned off by schemes worthy of Mr. Bernie Madoff?

Perhaps the most important question is: Why do so many of those same people think it is quite okay that we have thirty million citizens, mostly children and young people, who do not have any coverage at all? They have no insurance and are unable to get the medical and dental attention they need in the most important growing years of their life. One of the results is that these people who do not have insurance are flooding our emergency wards and resulting in large non-budgeted costs to the taxpayer.

Is it a matter that empathy and concern for thy fellow citizen is no longer one of the cornerstones of our society? Is it a result of the "me generation"? When it comes to sending monetary support to assist after natural or man made catastrophes outside our borders, there are usually no limits to our compassion, but why then are we so adamantly opposed to helping our own people?

And why are we so opposed to learning from other countries? We do not have to copy their system, but maybe we could learn something. There is no doubt that the high end of the American medical profession is second to none; that goes for the advancements and availability in equipment as well. The only two problems are that fewer and fewer people can afford that type of care, and the rest get no care at all. The health care of the American people is worse than that of most industrialized nations—at almost double the cost.

One of the biggest barriers to adopting something that was not invented here is that, in the red-blooded American mind, these other systems will open the doors to socialism and communism. So even though our system is broken and too expensive, it is ours (!) and it supports our capitalistic beliefs. We have to decide one day, though, if we really want to go down that road to the point where health care becomes so expensive that we can no longer afford it. At that time, something will hopefully be done, if it is not too late.

The problem with changing the current system with all its vested financial interests is that these very powerful entities stand to lose too much. Besides, actually doing some meaningful improvements to the system as it is would be like changing the tires on a speeding car.

There is yet another factor that has to be brought to the fore, which will put enormous pressures on the health care system-any health care system. This is the "obesity tsunami."

Although obesity is spreading to all corners of the world, courtesy of good, old, American fast food and lack of exercise, the U.S. is still the epicenter of the "fat fad." It is especially serious in the lower Mexico Gulf states, such as Alabama, Mississippi, and Louisiana. And it now starts with the children.

The added weight at such a young age already leads to early problems, such as cardiac troubles, high blood pressure, diabetes, and all kinds of other related illnesses, including heart attacks and strokes. The problem is more prevalent in families with limited income and less spending power per family member (i.e., families with many children). This is not surprising since these families will typically often buy cheap takeout food.

Food has to be prepared quickly because the head of the household works long hours, and thus does not have time to prepare dinner using a balanced food stock. Although more well-off people buy fast food or ready-made foods since they are also on a hectic daily treadmill, they can afford to buy certified organic and fat-free foods as well.

Or can they? Well, that should be one of the priorities of the government: to make sure that there is an abundance of healthy food available at an affordable cost. This may sound restrictive and incompatible with a so-called free economy, but if we wish to avoid a train wreck then it behooves us as a nation to do what can possibly be done to persuade (force?) the food producers to enter into collective agreements to produce and deliver healthy nourishment. This will entail stricter rules and regulations, and it will also require that nationwide kitchens for the kids in schools and colleges should be asked to change the menus to more nutritious food with restricted calories.

This will be a tough sell since these "soft" regulations will be regarded as attempts by government to control private matters for families and individuals. "Everyone should be allowed to eat what they want and as much as they want, and government should stay out of the kitchen" will be the message. But common sense dictates that some kind of awareness should be introduced of the magnitude of the issue and its trajectory toward an epidemic of heart problems of frightening proportions. The secretary of health should enlist the help of the secretary of education, as well as the media, to try to change people's eating habits, much like what was done to reduce the number of smokers. It's probably a long haul, but the sooner we get started, the sooner we will start to see the benefits in terms of better national health.

Exercise can help reduce the weight; however, today's society is very sedentary and young people are no longer forced to expend calories the old-fashioned way, by running on the playground, walking or cycling to school, and attending strict gym classes. Whereas their calorie intake has greatly increased as a result of larger, richer portions and frequent snacking, their movements have been largely eliminated. If they have to go somewhere, the car is usually the means of transportation, and when they are not sitting in the car, they will be found in front of the television or the PlayStation.

Once a young person reaches a certain weight threshold, exercise becomes at first arduous and difficult, and soon after that impossible, both mentally and physically. From there on out, trying to control the weight will become a lifelong losing battle, and it will have severe repercussions on feelings of well-being and self-confidence. Obesity is not only damaging to the health of the individual, but also to his or her happiness index.

If we do not control this obesity epidemic, we will, as a nation, implode on ourselves.

CHAPTER 23

Profiling-Legal?

YOU DO NOT pick a fight with the largest guy at the bar and you do not walk down a dark alley in the middle of the night. Why not? Because you have used your experience and deductive powers and have come to the conclusion that both of these circumstances could most likely be hazardous to your health. You have subconsciously carried out an evaluation of the possible risks based on what you have experienced and what you have heard and read. Your conclusion, which you arrive at almost instantaneously, is the end product of an evaluation in your subconscious using known parameters and handy templates created over years for situations such as these. These personal templates or filters make it easier and faster to make decisions and you do not have to "reinvent the wheel" every time you face a similar situation.

Is this "profiling"? When you shy away from eating yogurt, don't like liver, or prefer to watch baseball over football, you often characterize these choices as "preferences" or "selections." But when you feel uncomfortable with certain ethnic groups or you do not like people with high-pitched voices, you could rightfully label this as "profiling." What this means is that you will try to avoid these people based on their looks or their behavior. What is wrong with that?

There has been a lot of focus on this side of human behavior, mostly by individuals who have felt that their civil rights were violated. The phenomenon of "profiling" mostly, if not exclusively, occurs in connection with alleged illegal activity. It can be a state trooper stopping a car on the interstate freeway because he suspects the vehicle to have been stolen. He has a policeman's "hunch," which in that particular line of work is priceless, sometimes a life-saver. The car is pulled over and the driver is asked to present relevant papers, i.e., driver's license, car registration, and insurance. If everything is in order, the police tips his hat and wishes the driver a nice evening. If things are not okay and he finds that there might be criminal activity involved, he will go ahead and take appropriate action.

Now, here is the thing. If the driver with the infraction is a white person, there is not a problem. But if he happens to be black (African-American), there could be a big problem. The policeman may be accused of profiling, and this can lead to all kinds of ramifications and repercussions, such as a leave of absence for the trooper and maybe a lawsuit and favorable media coverage for the driver.

So what is the trooper to do-only stop white people and maybe Hispanics, but not other ethnic groups?.

The politically correct way of refraining from calling it profiling is to name it "random selection" using a predestined numerical order of checking. This will most often mean that an old lady in the check-in line at the airport will be taken aside for a complete body search just because the security that day works with numbers of ten and she happens to be the "lucky winner." And this in spite of the fact that right behind her stands the poster boy for international terrorism!

The question of profiling and alleged civil rights abuses was a key element for opponents of the Arizona law that was meant to clamp down on illegal immigrants. As most know, Arizona has a long border with Mexico, thus most of the illegals entering the state happen to be Mexicans. Therefore, when the police were given the mission of stopping any person under reasonable suspicion and ask for their immigration status, they would inevitably mostly stop Mexicans. There are not a lot of Canadians crossing the Mexican border. Likewise, there are not a lot of Caucasians coming north looking for a new and better life. Ergo, most of the people to be stopped would be Mexicans.

Arizona has only done what the federal government has failed to do: bar illegal immigrants from invading this country and expel the ones who are here illegally. This word, "illegal," has nothing to do with immigration. This has to do with the law, and the word "illegal" means just that: not legal.

The opponents of the law bring up the argument that the legal immigrants may also then be asked to prove their residency. So? If you are legal, why would you have any objections against showing proof that you are? In most other industrialized nations, this is not a problem.

It is only the ones who are here illegally who would object to showing proof of legal residency. And we are not just talking about hardworking people who want to send money back to their families. No, we are talking about an unhindered flow of drugs and criminals going north into this country and of guns and money going south to abet these criminals outside of our borders.

As everyone knows, this great land was built by immigrants and everyone's family tree shows the initial arrivals as immigrants looking to flee an oppressive regime or seek a better life. Most came of their own free will, by desire or necessity, and some came against their will as slaves. But all were immigrants and all became full-fledged members of the new world, America.

So how come this issue has become such a political hot potato? Is it because the politicians have all failed miserably to address this real and growing problem? You would think that such a modern and wealthy country like the U.S. could easily devise a program for handling immigration. This should take into account the various demands of the labor market, such as the seasonal demand for added farm workers, requirements for menial labor in the food processing industry, and the import of highly qualified scientists and engineers. And to use some common sense, a nationwide identification system would have to be introduced.

It is correct that decades of irresponsibility on the part of the lawmakers and presidents have resulted in twelve (an educated guess) million illegal or undocumented foreigners living in suspended existence and fear of being deported. The majority is from Mexico and Central America, but there are also scores of other nationalities. Occasionally the media will report on heartbreaking stories of families being fractured when one or more are caught and deported to their homeland. But illegal immigration is not a victimless crime. Every undocumented immigrant might take up space, which could otherwise be allocated to one of the legal residents, both in the job market and in the clinics, schools, and hospitals. The fact even that an illegal person can reap the benefits of a legal resident, such as schooling, obtaining a driver's license, and other public support is indeed a travesty and an affront to the legal immigrants.

It is often said in support of the illegal immigrants that our country needs them, that they do work otherwise shunned by citizens and legal residents, and that without them the whole of the California farming industry would suffer. That is a good argument for making a working immigration policy, one that takes these requirements into consideration. But it has to be done within the law and it has to be transparent. The practice of automatically issuing U.S. citizenship to the children born here by illegals must also stop immediately. How that practice ever became law is indeed a great mystery.

Some say in defense of the illegal immigrants that they do jobs that Americans will not do. This is a bogus reasoning, much like the cart before the horse. The willingness of American workers to do a job depends on how much that job pays—and the reason some jobs pay too little to attract citizens and legal residents is exactly the unfair competition from the poorly paid immigrants. This could be one reason the business community loves it the way it is!

Why do we not see fining, prosecuting, or otherwise punishing of those U.S. employers who flout the law by knowingly hiring illegal immigrants? Could this be because the political establishment has guaranteed these companies a lifelong membership in the "get out of jail free" club?

Even if those being caught and deported have otherwise led an exemplary life with jobs and family, they are still criminals because they are here illegally. In the debate by the politicians and in the reports by the media, it is never mentioned that there are close to five million citizens and lawful residents who are applying for visas for their families and dependents. Most of these are still waiting, sometimes decades after having submitted the applications and paid the fees at every step of the process.

The fact that so much energy is spent by the press on the issue of illegal immigrants totally overshadows the plight of the legal immigrants and the whole visa system. It is a serious affront to all legal immigrants, who have spent years and money going through the proper channels as required, that the illegal immigrants are treated as victims.

The whole focus on illegal immigrants has unfortunately had the effect that the legal immigration process as a whole has gotten bogged down in a bureaucratic quagmire. The rules are onerous, the waits are almost like life sentences, and the service is nonexistent. If it were not so serious for the applicants, it would be almost laughable. (This could have catastrophic effects for the future of the high-end technology firms and entrepreneurial start-ups since the intellectual brains floating around in the world will not be able to find a home in the U.S.)

All of this is forgotten in the debate. Instead of spending so much time on what is wrong, there should be a serious effort exerted by the politicians to sort this out and come up with a workable solution. As stated before, this is not rocket science. But, unfortunately, a possible solution has been caught in the tentacles of party politics in Washington, D.C.

It is amazing how Newton's law of gravity can seemingly depend on party affiliation! If a Democrat were to state that the sun is shining, the Republican would refuse to look out the window. This sometimes reminds us of two boys on the playground arguing over whose father is the biggest and strongest.

This is a sad state of affairs indeed, as none of the nation's most pressing problems will be addressed in a common-sense and logical manner. The petrification on both sides of the aisle has led to an unbridgeable chasm the width of the Grand Canyon. One can think back with some veneration to the "good old days" when deals were made in smoke-filled back rooms. But, of course, now that smoking has been banned, these sessions can no longer take place!

The immigration situation, which is dire for everyone outside the Beltway, needs to be addressed, discussed, negotiated, and decided upon as a high-priority matter. The selfish posturing and concern about whether one is reelected is strangling any attempts to be proactive and innovative. Only one thought guides the politicians in their daily work, and that is not to say or do anything that might upset their constituents and thus their chances of being reelected. That is an insurmountable impediment to deciding on the essential steps that have to be taken to maintain and bring this nation forward.

They could start by enforcing the laws already on the books. Without enforcement, there is no law.

Even though America has one of the highest fertility rates in the world and will therefore be able to fuel the economic development with "home-grown workers," the country needs a lot more hands to carry the prosperity forward, especially ones with special high-end skills, like engineers, scientists, and researchers. This means that immigration is a crucial element in the whole debate about future growth. In addition, America is known for the ease with which it assimilates new arrivals, although that reputation is getting some-what singed at the edges (especially with Spanish-speaking immigrants failing to make an effort to learn English). This makes it increasingly problematical for integration and, as mentioned earlier, will lead to a Balkanization of the country. And history has clearly documented what happened to the Balkans.

Instead of debating the real problem of illegal immigration affecting all of the U.S., although some states more than others, someone has turned the whole matter on its head by bringing up some civil rights issues concerning the elusive concept of "profiling." Illegal immigrants cover all nationalities from all over the world. This problem is not limited to Mexicans. There are also Russians, Chinese, Nigerians, etc. It is well known that many visitors to the U.S. on student visas, au pair assignments, and other limited-time visas will "disappear" into the general populace as illegals.

As strange as it might look, the lawmakers in Washington and the ad-ministration all want to sink the Arizona immigration initiative while the overwhelming majority of voters in the U.S. think it is a good idea. While the U.S. Justice Department is moving to kill it before it spreads, other states in the union may introduce the same or similar measures. Who do the "Beltway Bandits" represent?

Most people have probably forgotten that Arizona already signed a bill in 2007 aimed at stemming the tide of illegal immigrants from the other side of the border. The current secretary of the U.S. Department of Homeland Security, Janet Napolitano, as the then-governor of Arizona signed a bill that prohibits people from knowingly hiring illegal immigrants and requires businesses to verify applicants' employment eligibility. She said at that time that Arizona had to act out of necessity because Congress "finds itself incapable of coping with the comprehensive immigration reforms our country needs." Now there is a new governor but nothing else has changed; the message is the same: We have to secure our borders against an invasion.

Strangely enough, this is the one area where all of the senators agree. So why not adopt the modular approach to this legislation? A comprehensive immigration reform simply has provisions too contentious to command a majority of Congress or the country. Why not concentrate first on closing the border to illegal contraband, people, guns, drugs, and crime? Since everyone agrees that this has the highest priority, all they have to do is approve a sufficient budget and a "building plan." Instead of applying the usual government acquisition rules, whereby the low bidder is awarded the contract, this work should be awarded on best value and with no influence by lobbyists. With the low bidder, you usually end up with an inferior product and huge cost overruns.

Once the tidal wave is stemmed, the problem of illegal contraband will have been minimized, if not eliminated. It will then be a lot easier for Congress to address the remaining parts, including amnesty, seasonal working permits and national ID cards. This would make a lot of sense indeed—common sense.

In addition to the immigration legislation, there are also other important issues such as the education of our young people, renewal of inner cities, job creation in an increasingly competitive world, transportation infrastructure, and a modern health care system. These are just some of the important points, but without the willingness to address them in a non-partisan manner, nothing will be done. Do the politicians even care?

Why don't they use some common sense in the approach to solving these problems in a straightforward manner? Look at it like a contractor building a high-rise. There are many ways in which the design and execution can be handled, but if there is only talk, the high-rise will not be built. It will all be hot air without walls.

CHAPTER 24

Live and Let Live

IN AMERICA, CERTAIN groups are committing murder under the guise of wanting to save lives.

These groups are carrying out terrorism in the belief that they have the divine right to murder other people. And they murder people whom they do not know and for people who don't even exist!

We are, of course, talking about the extreme wing of the "Right to Life" members, who in their own minds are convinced that they have been ordained to be the ultimate arbiters of life and death-in other words, they "play God."

The subject is abortion. Many people, especially in the U.S., have strong opinions that abortion means saving mothers by killing babies. The issue has become quite contentious as it pits the rights of the individual to decide over her own body against the rights of a fertilized egg. The decision of the woman who has become impregnated is challenged by strangers with no vested interest or familiarity with the pregnant woman. These total strangers have cloaked themselves in the righteous cape of supreme morality and see it as their ethical duty to prevent any woman from making this serious decision involving her own body.

Abortion is truly a serious matter, especially for the pregnant woman, and it is one that is not treated lightly. It is therefore disturbing that this woman who is already suffering from heart wrenching emotions and life altering decisions also has to endure the threats and verbal abuse from people she does not know and who do not know her. This mental battering and psychological bullying by total strangers constitutes real terror.

A woman's right to an abortion was achieved through a landmark decision by the Supreme Court in *Roe v. Wade* in 1973. The following is a quote from WIKIPEDIA (the free encyclopedia):

Roe v. Wade, 410 U.S. 113 (1973), was a landmark decision by the United States Supreme Court on the issue of abortion. The court held that the woman's right to an abortion is determined by the stage of pregnancy, and the state cannot prohibit abortion before viability. After viability, the state cannot prohibit abortion if abortion "is necessary, in appropriate medical judgment, for the preservation of the life or health of the mother" as defined in the companion case of Doe v Bolton. The Court said that "viability" means potentially able to live outside the mother's womb, albeit with artificial aid. Viability is usually placed at about seven months (28 weeks) but may occur earlier, even at 24 weeks.

The Court rested these conclusions on a constitutional right to privacy emanating from the Due Process Clause of the Fourth Amendment, also known as substantive due process.

It has therefore been established that women have an inalienable right to an abortion. This right, however, has not been accepted by some of the "Right to Life" members, who are seemingly oblivious to the fact that the U.S. is a country based on the Constitution and legally binding interpretations by the Supreme Court.

In a constitutional democracy, they have every right to seek to change the laws, again through the democratic process. As they only represent a relatively small part of the overall population, this will probably not happen, so they have resorted to doing everything else in their power to impede the procedure.

These efforts range all the way from amending state constitutions, to adding "bureaucratic roadblocks" for women seeking abortions, to actually removing abortion facilities, either by torching the clinics or killing the doctors performing the surgeries. The idea here is that if they can remove the clinics and the doctors, it will be impossible for most women to get an abortion. The irony is that the women who need the abortion the most (the poor and the young) are the ones suffering most from these obstructions. In many states in the Union politicians swayed by the militant anti-abortion groups have introduced a number of laws which without constituting a direct ban on abortion have managed to make abortion impossible. This has been done by attaching rules to the certification of abortion doctors and their practices which are so onerous that they cannot possible be met.

It defies common sense that these extremist "Right to Lifers" are able to terrorize with impunity the rights of women across the country, rights which have been guaranteed by the Constitution. Apart from being a serious criminal issue, it also threatens the health of women all over this land.

Citizens of this country do not have the right to murder their fellow citizens just because they happen not to agree with them.

As an aside another industrialized nation, in this case France voted to fully reimburse all abortions and to make contraception free for those between 15 and 18. National medical insurance currently pays in full for abortions for minors and the poor, while other women are reimbursed for up to 80 % of the procedure's cost, which can be as much as $ 580. Contraception is partially reimbursed. Why can this not be introduced in the U.S.?

*In America, so many men are against abortion.
Are they afraid they will ever get one?*

CHAPTER 25

Energy-From Where?

THE RECENT CATASTROPHIC oil spill in the Gulf of Mexico has finally opened people's eyes to the inherent dangers of extracting the basic energy stock from the earth, be it coal, gas, or oil. In addition to the spill, there have been numerous coal-mining accidents lately with loss of life.

Apart from the enormity of the spill in the Gulf, which was quite unprecedented, extracting coal and oil has always had its perils, and accidents have happened. One of the differences between now and years ago is that there are many more active sites and news travels at the speed of light.

The catastrophe in the Gulf revealed a glaring problem between industry and the government agencies tasked with ensuring that they operate in a failsafe manner.

Not that long ago we witnessed what happened when a government agency, the Securities and Exchange Commission (SEC), sadly failed to enforce the federal securities laws and regulations. They absconded from their duties and we all know the result it had in the financial world-and in our real world.

Here again was another government agency, this time the Mineral Management Services (MMS), an agency of the United States Department of the Interior that manages the nation's natural gas, oil, and other mineral resources on the outer continental shelf (OCS). The MMS is responsible for inspection and oversight of energy companies to ensure they are following the law and protecting the safety of their workers and the environment.

There is, of course, always a conflict of interests built into a system where the government agency enforcing the rules is also the beneficiary of the payments by the company they are inspecting. This incestuous relationship often leads to a weakening of the oversight and to an unhealthy strengthening of the "personal relationships" between the enforcer and his client.

There is no doubt that MMS should have insisted on verifiable and proven cut-off systems for the well head in case of problems. Only when thorough testing of concept and components had been certified should a permit have been issued to the oil company. It is the order of the day in most other engineering projects that a failure analysis be conducted. With systems such as this exploration rig working at great depths, there should have been back-up plans and contingency plans, much like when NASA sends an expensive rocket into space. Here there was not even the most rudimentary plan for "what if?" And, again, we know all too well what happened to our world with this spill!

This is akin to the unsinkable cruise liner, the *Titanic*, on which nobody had done a failure and consequence analysis of what would happen if the outer hull were breached. Consideration should have been given to spacing watertight bulkheads such that there would have been adequate margins for even unthinkable damages. And in the unthinkable event that she did sink, there should certainly have been lifeboats for all (Plan B).

What the catastrophe in the Gulf of Mexico also revealed was that ordinary people have very little knowledge of what makes the TV turn on, where the energy comes from, and how it's generated.

The media tries to distill years of engineering know-how and operating experience into sound bites, experts' opinions, and panel discussions. When, for instance, oceanographers are invited to explain a simulated model of future oil flow in the ocean, they have no time to explain all the variables. So what is just one of many possible scenarios is being absorbed by the public as the gospel truth.

It is no wonder that these matters are hard to understand. It usually takes a four-year college degree and a lot of years of learning the practical applications before one has enough knowledge to fully appreciate the nature of the problem. And even then it does not guarantee that one can solve the problem. The mere fact that so many people in connection with the oil spill in the Gulf of Mexico suggested, in earnest, that the U.S. government should take over the job of plugging the well from BP shows that they had no idea of the nature of this problem. Even though it was explained numerous times that the U.S. government does not possess the instruments and the expertise to remedy the situation, many people still urged the government to kick BP out and take over.

They even went so far as to demand that the president put himself in charge and solve the problem. And when the president time after time reminded people that BP was the only entity that could fix this calamity, he was accused of relinquishing his obligations as the nation's leader, and they went so far as to insinuate that he was weak and not in charge. Well, he was very much in charge, but much like any house owner who must leave the bug decontamination of his dwelling to an outside contractor, so here did the president give the job to the only contractor capable of solving the problem.

Again it showed that the listeners and the viewers had no idea of the difficulties that would be encountered in trying to cap the well spewing oil into the Gulf. People's efforts and focus on the protection of the shores and animal life, as well as on the cleanup of the oil already in the ocean, was well placed. So was their frustration over the lack of urgency with which this work was being approached by the government. The U.S. government, in the form of the U.S. Coast Guard (USCG), was already working closely with BP and applying pressure on them to perform. As an arm of government, USCG is in charge of the safety of all sea-borne vessels in U.S. waters, and as such already had the authority to act as enforcer. They furthermore possess the engineering capability, which meant they could partake in the ongoing technical discussions carried out. There was a slight problem with the shared responsibility between USCG and MMS. Where USCG is responsible for everything above and on the surface of the water, MMS has responsibility for what happens on the sea floor.

It would have been a great help, both in defusing the anger of people across the country and of helping the president and his staff, if the media had spent more time trying to explain how difficult such an operation really was instead of constantly (every hour!) emphasizing that things ought to happen faster.

There is no doubt at all that this was a catastrophic spill, one that will be felt for a long time by the fishing and tourist businesses in the whole coastal area. The damage to the wildlife and their habitat may also be irreparable. So what started as frustration and fear soon turned to anger when the problem could not be solved quickly.

Common sense says that some problems take longer than others to solve. The oil spill in the Gulf of Mexico was visible and became a constant reminder of an ever-present danger. Other problems, like the health care crisis, breakdown of the democratic process, and the national debt, are less visible and more visceral, but just as dangerous.

As the U.S. is evolving into a much more flexible and complex society, one that could almost be called "liquid," we have to develop more collective resilience to the momentary setbacks and frequent catastrophes that are unavoidable consequences of the speed of evolution and the forces of nature. It's like a young boy running on the pavement at great speed. He will fall and scrape his knees and elbows, but after some tears and a kind word from his mother, he starts running again and soon picks up speed. So it should be with our reactions to the misfortunes happening around us.

Grief and sorrow have their places, but we have to be careful that they do not lead to fear and paralysis.

Unfortunately, rather than only reporting on the disasters, the media today seem to be thriving off them. They keep stoking the fires in an attempt to keep the viewers' attention and their sponsors' air-time requirements.

There should also be that "kind word from the mother" so we can move on, away from the tears. Although good news is seldom newsworthy, the collective media should feel some kind of duty to be unbiased and balanced-in other words, to get us back and running again. It is well-known that we are more fascinated by a burning building than by pictures of a lovely meadow, and the media is catering to our "burning" desires.

———

With this, let us return to the question of energy! There's a lot of talk about alternate energy sources: solar, biomass, wind, and wave energy. Some have stated that these sources will replace oil, gas, and coal in the foreseeable future, within the next ten to twenty years. This just goes to show again that these people are totally out of touch with reality. They have no idea of how much we rely on these present energy sources. Oil, for instance, drives the whole world's fleet of ships, tankers, container ships, tug boats, ferries, and so on. It would be very hard to imagine how this energy source could come from wind turbines or solar power in the foreseeable future.

And then there are the petrochemical industries that also rely on carbon products. Certainly wind power would not be an easy substitute.

Common sense tells us that we have to be realistic. It makes sense to include all potential sources of energy to play a role in the future energy scenario. Like a piano player using all the keys and a painter using the full range of colors, we also have to look at all the possible sources, including new technology. A lot of research and engineering has to be funded to develop the alternative methods, lifespan production costs have to be assessed, and ways of distribution evaluated. One could argue that we should try to fund this effort partly through taxation of existing energy sources. This leads to the question of costs.

Everyone feels good when they talk about "green energy," "renewable energy," and "carbon-free footprints," but no one mentions that this comes at a cost, especially when one looks at the cost per kW or BTU. As long as we are aware that there are costs and trade-offs, we can discuss it in an open and transparent manner. There are no "free lunches." Also, there has to be an acknowledgment that the present energy production, be it from oil, gas, or coal, is very efficient measured in dollars per kW delivered, or, as you could say, "from well to user." It will be a lot of years before alternate energy providers will reach similar levels, also taking into account the amortization of the development and research costs.

The challenge for the U.S. president is to create an energy forum that will not be influenced by the interests of the powerful oil and gas lobby, while at the same time realizing the importance of oil and gas. The American public has to be informed that oil, gas, and coal are beneficial to us and to our lives, and that they will be around for a very long time to come. Even renewable energy comes at a cost, apart from the initial investment costs. There is also the upkeep and the repairs and maintenance costs, which even for a wind turbine is not zero.

It would be a good idea for the U.S. government to plant the seeds by funding basic research and development (R&D) like they did for the Internet and for biotechnology. After the kick start by the government, private enterprise and venture capitalists can do what they do best, namely expand and commercialize the technology. The U.S. cannot afford to lose this new race for alternate energy sources and associated spinoffs. There is no doubt that this technology will be a major employer—provided that we strengthen our science and engineering education (as mentioned earlier).

The alternate energy sources should be matured over the years to become commercially viable substitutes to oil and gas wherever possible. This commercialization could be accelerated with incentives through grants, tax breaks, and favorable loans by the government. It must be remembered that this is a cost to the tax payer.

While we are striving to replace some of our present energy sources with alternate energy, we should not forget that unless we reduce our overall rate of increase in consumption, these new energy sources will not make much of an impact.

We should therefore consider "energy conservation" as an "alternate energy source."

Refraining from using plastic water bottles by refilling used bottles with tap water and using knapsacks for goods in the supermarket are two measures that save a huge amount of oil. All plastic products, many of the materials used to make the clothes we wear, or the carpet we walk on, plus hundreds of other products we take for granted are made from petrochemicals. As the name implies, a main ingredient in petrochemicals is oil. They also have the added benefits of not requiring investments and of leaving no carbon footprints.

There are also energy-reducing measures, such as insulating one's home and using energy-efficient appliances. The payback on the investment is short and, again, there's no carbon footprint.

We should also not forget the food chain. Producing animal protein requires eight times as much fossil fuel as producing a comparable amount of plant protein. So, if we could convince this great meat-eating nation to cut back as a matter of habit, we will save great amounts of oil consumption and import.

In 2015, the United States imported approximately 9.4 million barrels per day (MMb/d) of petroleum from about 82 countries. Petroleum includes crude oil, natural gas plant liquids, liquefied refinery gases, refined petroleum products such as gasoline and diesel fuel, and biofuels including ethanol and biodiesel. About 78% of gross petroleum imports were crude oil.

In 2015, the United States exported about 4.8 MMb/d of petroleum to 136 countries. Most of the exports were petroleum products. The resulting net imports (imports minus exports) of petroleum were about 4.6 MMb/d. (U.S. Energy Information Administration)

As can be seen we still import a large part of our oil products consumption from foreign sources. This means that we are dependent on foreign oil and as a consequence extremely vulnerable both as regards delivery and price. Some of the countries we deal with are not very stable politically and their reserves are finite after all. It goes without saying that we have tailored our foreign policy as a part of our national security agenda to secure adequate delivery of oil. It is therefore essential that we everything in out power to reduce domestic consumption.

Feeding Frenzy
Feeding Who?

CHAPTER 26

Debt Economy

Is it a healthy economic system that promotes the illusion of creation of wealth just by rearranging it?

IT IS NOT the intention here to repeat what has already been covered by the media about the reasons for and the consequences of the recent financial crises in the U.S.A. and the rest of the world. Anybody who does not know by now why the implosion happened and what the results have been must have spent a long time in a secluded place.

The official reason for the financial collapse is that funds were allocated based on assets grossly overvalued, and financial instruments selling debt were structured in such a way that decision makers and watchdogs had no way of understanding their potential risk to the whole system. And to top it off, this unknown risk was backed by insurance!

This should remind us of an old burger ad for Wendy's, where a little old lady with her chin on the counter yells in frustration, "Where's the beef?" This is a different take on the well-known fairy tale by the Danish writer and poet Hans Christian Andersen. His tale, "The Emperor's New Clothes," is about two weavers who promise an emperor a new suit of clothes invisible to those incompetent or unfit for their positions. When the emperor parades before his subjects in his new clothes (which had been made of air), a child cries out, "But he isn't wearing anything at all!"

Both of these examples make the point that you should always look for the substance behind the claims. It is not always that easy for ordinary people to assess whether the goods being peddled are real or fake. But it always pays to use one's common sense, and if it sounds too good to be true, it probably is. This was especially true in the recent financial crises where ordinary people could not rely on experts and government watchdogs. This was indeed a wake up call for the ordinary usually trusting citizen.

It's a different story when you talk about the so-called "experts": the real estate agents, fund managers, bank executives, and government watchdogs. They should have been very well equipped to evaluate the real value and the risk of transactions in their field of expertise. It is rather amazing, and a testament to the powers of mass suggestive media coverage, that the whole nation, save a few "courageous individuals," did believe that "what goes up never comes down" and that the underlying weakness could be glossed over by enough euphoria (lipstick!) to make it appear to be what it wasn't. Everyone wanted a cabin on the *Titanic*-icebergs be damned!

So, we capitalized profits and socialized failures, bailing out banks and managing to reward those people who had caused the crisis with huge bonuses. This was widely regarded by "Main Street America" as an affront to their hard work, sacrifices, and suffering. To fuel the economy and get people back to work, the government decided to pump money into the banking system, thus freeing up funds for loans. This was common sense; however, it did not quite work as intended. The banks said, "Thank you very much!" and kept the money to boost their reserves. The excuse for not lending to small business owners, entrepreneurs, and new house buyers was that it would be too risky in this volatile financial climate!

In spite of the insult of this self-serving attitude, they were right on one point, namely that the economy is extremely volatile. Not enough has been said about the real threat to economic recovery and it's almost as if we dare not bring it up. This "big elephant in the room" is, of course, the national debt. It has been mentioned from time to time, but serious efforts to properly explain the danger of this debt, which at this time (2010) is in excess of thirteen trillion U.S. dollars and counting, has failed to rouse the interest of the ordinary person. Maybe it is difficult to understand, but those who recall 1992 presidential candidate Ross Perot will remember his very simple charts on TV explaining to the American voters the differences between national debt and national deficit, as well as other macro financial parameters. Although it is expected to top $17.6 trillion by late 2016, the national debt has dropped out of the headlines recently. Out of sight may indeed mean out of mind, especially in Washington, but that hardly means the problem has gone away — as a new report from the Congressional Budget Office makes clear.

With unemployment foremost on people's minds, it behooves the administration to make the effort to explain the whole equation, "U.S. Budget 101." Only then will people be ready to make the sacrifices needed to improve the long-term situation. Common sense says to take the medicine now in order to be healthy later. It has to be explained that the budget consists of mandatory expenses and discretionary expenses. The mandatory expenses cover Social Security, Medicare, Medicaid, and interest on national debt, and these consume most all of the national income in the form of taxes and other revenues.

Medicare is being taken hostage to political demagoguery. In discussing the enormous debt the country is suffering under and ways of reducing this burden some politicians are using this fiscal problem to try to eliminate the government health care systems, Medicare and Medicaid. This proposal to replace the government run care with private health care options is done in the name of cost saving much like the wolf dons a coat of sheep skin to fool the masses.

The two programs, Medicare and Medicaid are both serving the elderly exceptionally well, and efficiently. It is probably true as has been alleged that there is a lot of fraud going on which weighs on the cost of the programs. Solving this problem should not be done by closing it down. This would be akin to selling your car and buying a new one just because there were some problems with the exhaust system.

The concept works wonders for the elderly in this country, however like all programs it needs to be tweaked from time to time and a more intensive effort has to be made to implement strict cost control. Any persons or organizations fraudulently using the system for own gains should be harshly dealt with.

U.S. citizens are generally well-thinking, level-headed people who are quite familiar with household budgeting. So common sense tells them that in order to bridge the gap between expenses and income, you can increase the income, cut expenses, or borrow some more (the last of which you can only do for a limited time). For most people, the income side is locked in, but the government is in a better position since it has the power to raise taxes.

The main thing to remember is that, when consumer spending is down, business is going to lay people off rather than hire them. So, the vicious cycle starts: spending down, less production, less employment, spending down… The only way out of this "employment quicksand" is for the government to step in and spend, pay unemployment insurance, and give tax breaks to people who will spend or increase their payroll. Tax breaks should not be given to the rich, most of whom have managed not to pay any taxes to speak of, using the tax code to their advantage. And giving money to the wealthy does not necessarily lead to more money being spent on consumption or investment. It is a fallacy, as also pointed out by Thomas Piketty in his book, "CAPITAL in the Twenty-First Century", that the rich in America are job creators. More and more of their wealth is derived from assets they own and from inheritance, not from being entrepreneurs.

It is also essential that the banks start assuming their role in society, which is that of lending to worthy causes and hardworking people. The banks' charter, after all, is to lend money and fuel the economy, not to siphon necessary funds out of the economy to boost their own reserves. We should not forget that the banks borrow money at lower rates than their lending rates; thus, their money "machine" is well-oiled. Lack of credit strangles small companies as it kills their cash flow. Most small businesses rely on a bank credit, a credit line to bridge the time gap between the purchasing of raw materials and the receipt of sales receivables. If they are unable to pay their suppliers, they will not receive the goods needed to maintain their production. It is not very difficult to see where this is headed.

It is a sobering fact that less and less of the available capital is "at work" in industry. It is estimated that only 15 % of the money is being used in business. The rest is being circulated in the financial money machine, from stock buy-back, mergers and acquisitions and investments. This incestuous insider circulation of liquidity is sucking the oxygen out of the entrepreneurial room and new business start-ups are being starved for capital. Increasingly large companies are beginning to act as financial institutions, where the profits are made on paper instead of on production.

In addition to causing terrible damage to our competitiveness as a nation, the increased number of unemployed will cause unspeakable pain at the human level. Long-term unemployment has shown to result in apathy, anger, despair, illness, alcoholism, and the breakup of families. For a lot of younger people who may not even get a chance to enter the job market, they will be left with nowhere to go but the street corner. In the following chapter, "USA the land of opportunity", the livable wage issue is discussed in more detail.

Changes also need to be carried out on the tax code. Common sense tells us that in order to make the system of taxation fair and equitable, taxes should be paid according to ability, not inclination. This will mean a "flat tax rate" for all, with the exception that less able people will not pay tax and rich people should pay a higher rate. The rich should pay more because they can; more importantly, their interests are best served when society is well funded and productive. See the section, "Taxes – Foundation"

In order to build and maintain a society with a high "happiness index," we have to start thinking about the following saying:

We should be <u>feeding</u> one another—not <u>feeding off</u> one another!

CHAPTER 27

U.S.A. – The land of opportunity?

THE OLD ADAGE that everyone can make it in America is beginning to loose its luster. "If we work harder we can ensure a better life for our children". This used to be the driver up through the early part of the new century. Driven by the market forces after the last world war a huge manufacturing base grew out of the war machine filling a market hungry for products such as cars, washing machines, TV's and all the other new gadgets flooding the market in those early years. And of course the ultimate wish for most families was a car and a house in a nice neighborhood with a garden and a dog. America became the supermarket, hardware store and auto dealership to the world. Markets for American products abounded and opportunity was everywhere for American workers of all economic means to get ahead. America had a virtual monopoly on rebuilding the world. Combined with the G.I. Bill of 1944, which provided money for returning veterans to go to college, and government loans to buy houses and start businesses, the middle class in America boomed, as did American power, wealth and prestige.

The production sector was busy and jobs were plentiful. And the salaries were such as they had never been before. This in turn enabled the normal citizen to become a consumer of goods and services and once the critical mass was reached where consumption and production were feeding off one another the great gravy train was off and running.

There were still poor and disadvantaged people who had missed the train, but they were in a minority. Most people were working and making enough money to maintain a life style with an upwards momentum. Students did not have to worry about getting a job after high school or college and the cost of the college education could be paid off relatively quickly. Most of the larger companies had generous health care plans and more and more of these also offered retirement plans for their employees. In those days they were called "Defined benefit plans", and they gave the people a certain assurance that they would be all right in their sunset years.

This growing part of the American consumerism was supported by what was more and more often referred to as the "Middle Class". The general understanding was that this class of people was made up of workers in manufacturing, offices and services who were gainfully employed, sufficiently paid with the financial power to keep the consumerism's wheel turning at a pleasant clip. They were comfortable and they were not worried about the future. The future looked bright both for them and for their kids. There seemed to have been a healthy relationship between the number of high school graduates and college bound students. Apprenticeships were not difficult to come by and a college degree was not a must in order to get a well paying job.

This was the time where the wealthy Americans were not so conspicuous. Sure they were there and their lives would occasionally make the headlines but there were not that many. This was before sportsmen and performers were receiving today's astronomically obscene remunerations. Most of the wealth at that time had been generated through manufacturing, trading, executive management positions or as had been the norm for centuries, by inheritance.

There was a feeling of opportunity for all, a feeling that the sky was the limit and that America was the "Promised Land" where everyone could find financial security and a purpose of life.

During the last decade and a half the American dream has evaporated, jobs have been disappearing or downgraded and the future looks like it's not going to materialize for an ever increasing number of Americans. What happened? Well, many factors came together to create a "perfect storm". On the international macro side, the rest of the world caught up to the U.S. and manufacturing jobs has been seeping out over a period of 30 – 40 years, textiles, cars, toys and a myriad of electronics products. Production in many other countries, predominantly the Far East has been able to produce at lower cost. Labor costs were lower and the cost of doing business in those countries has also been significantly lower, since stringent labor safety measures and environmental protections did not play a role. In order to compete many American based product lines have also been moved overseas thus further eroding the resident production base and the requirement for factory labor.

And then there was the crash in the housing market described in the previous chapter. When the bubble burst trillions of dollars held by ordinary Americans vanished overnight, and there was no one who could bail them out. This wealth that had all of for sudden been wiped out represented safe retirement, college educations, mobility and last but not least housing. With one fatal blow the middle class got decimated and fear of the future became real.

The banks were saved through government intervention, however they were shell shocked enough to start hoarding cash to the detriment of small businesses and merchants who were deeply dependent on loans to ensure credits and cash flow. This squeeze on liquidity caused a further set back with the recovery from the crash. Larger corporations were also cash caution and investments and expansions were delayed.

This shock treatment left the whole system traumatized, so when industry recovered and earnings started improving, this positive development did not produce a corresponding earnings flow downwards in the system. Apart from the executive floors where salaries were exploding and bonuses ballooned there was no move to increase the salary of the ordinary employee. On the contrary, if the company had the opportunity to go non-union or to hire in lower salaried new comers this would be a preferred way of increasing the bottom line – and thus management's bonus payment. So, for the last ten years most salaries have been stagnant, which of course means that in real terms, taking the cost of living into consideration the salaries in today's dollars have decreased.

The politicians all talk about the "employment numbers". Any sign that these are going up is interpreted as a sign that more and more people are better off. That is not so! You have to look at the hourly wage and whether this is a sustainable wage or not. Because of the stagnant wages and the rigid wage structure many people have resorted to having multiple jobs just to be able to feed their family. The number of new-hires in any given period is not an indicator of the health of a society. One should count the number of new employees in the job market who could actually afford to be self sustained, without resorting to food stamps or low income housing.

One can look at the wage stagnation as an intentional shift of society's cost away from the employers to the state. By keeping salaries suppressed the companies will increase their profit, however the cost of feeding and clothing the families has now been transferred to the social services in terms of food stamps, housing vouchers and subsidized child care. In short, the companies make more profit and the tax payers foot the bill! And of course a more important effect which is not often emphasized is the fact that by limiting the income of the ordinary worker you are also stifling the buying power of the general public; in other words the consumption goes down and that in turn has a direct consequence for the sales of products and services. This is an evil circle all driven by the absence of a living wage.

This has finally led to a nationwide discussion of whether a "Minimum wage" should be mandated. This discussion will hopefully result in serious debate as to what this will entail both as it relates to wage pressure on smaller merchants, restaurants and mom-and-pop stores as well as how it will lift people out of the poverty pool and reduce the cost of social services. It must be remembered though that although a basic concept can be adapted to the nation as a whole, the actual minimum wage levels should be set at levels reflecting the cost of living at each state, city and community. The cost of living in San Francisco is substantially higher than the cost of living say in Knoxville, Tennessee, and the wage structure has to take this into account.

The unfortunate result of this renewed debate on a "living wage" is that it is being regarded by many of the elite and leaders of industry to be a "socialist ploy" in line with "free education", "paid maternity leave" and "a single payer health care system". Just the mentioning of a more balanced social contract, something which could help reduce the inequality in the U.S. gets the conservative politicians the jitters and they start throwing words around such as "Socialism" and "Marxism" in order to paint a scary picture of red banners, Gulags and institutionalized poverty in the name of equality. Little do they realize that social democracies have ruled in most European industrialized nations for over a century, and that maybe – just maybe America could learn a thing or two about how to generate a more equal society. The institutionalized inequality in the U.S. has taken on epic proportions, where a very small minority owns over half of the nation's wealth. Much of this wealth has been amassed not through manufacturing and trade but through investments, i.e. the wealth they own – and inheritance. Income through wealth, i.e. dividend, capital gains and interests is not taxed as highly as income earned through labor, i.e. wages and salaries. And since wealth begets more wealth the growth is exponential.

Furthermore, to add insult to injury wealth begets power. In an American electoral system which runs on donations, money is power; and now even more so with the Supreme Court's ruling "Citizens United", which unleashed a Tsunami of unlimited financial support from corporate entities. Our founding fathers had structured the United States Constitution with what they saw as sufficient checks and balances to obtain a balanced society away from the shackles of a "Old world" Royal regime. Little did they know that their carefully drafted language is now been construed to allow for a system quite similar – an Privileged Class.

This privileged top part of the population is increasingly acting as a segregated part of society, like a different social order. This results in a more and more isolated class of self contained and self sustainable groupings of citizens with an ever increasing social-economic and political power. The dynamics of that chosen group are focused inward in a self perpetuating almost incestuous drive towards furthering their own interests and separating themselves from the less fortunate. None of their wealth and social qualities are seen to benefit the rest of society as these are harnessed in the reinforcement of their own position and expanding influence.

As these "chosen" people have few interactions with the middle class and the lower class their understanding of the everyday struggles of those segments of society are dismal at best; consequently they lack the appreciation of the importance of social assistance programs and the daily struggles of poor and middle class families in the US when it comes to health, jobs, education and housing. The absence of social empathy amongst this elite group is crucial as that same group has a great deal of influence on the legislative process thanks to their wealth and political affiliations.

This stratification of our society with a growing elite distancing themselves from the rest threatens to upset the fabric of our democracy where fairness and equal opportunity is such an essential part of what we are as a people and as a nation – or used to be(?).

CHAPTER 28

Taxes – The Necessary Foundation

THE WORD "TAX" is a word which is often associated with loss, pain and secret men in long coats and dark sunglasses - and it can lead to heart palpitations for even the most righteous and law abiding citizen. But the word describes the foundation for a well-functioning democratic society with modern infrastructure and shared services. There are a myriad of different taxes, on income, capital gains, property etc. but the common thread is that these "taxes" constitutes society's income from which all the goods and services are being paid. And the idea is that the system be constructed such that it is fair and equal, i.e. that each and every member of society is paying taxes according to that person's capability.

The revenue collected as taxes is the income side of the budget, where the expense side consist of everything from infrastructure maintenance like roads, power plants, parks, rails and waterways to social benefits like social security payments for retired people, hospitals, schools and defense like navy, air force and army and last but not least salary for all of the people working in the public sector, teachers, mail men, fire fighters and civil servants, just to name a few.

For a country like the U.S.A. this operating budget is huge indeed. It is broken down into federal, state- city and individual municipalities, where each entity is responsible for making certain that there is enough money for a safe and sound long term operation of that state, city and municipality.

The picture has been somewhat abridged just to illustrate how simple this mechanism really is. There are of course further parts of the budgeting process such as funding of long term obligations to worker's pensions, accruals for pending future planned work and set-asides for unexpected expenditures, i.e. for firefighting, snow removal and natural catastrophes. But all in all the funds for operating the system of goods and services for the benefit of all is paid for by taxing all. Well, at least that's the idea – but that is not how it works in real life.

Some recent news articles have pointed to the ever increasing tax evasion actions taken by large, profitable US companies. The Boeing Co. extorted the Washington State for an amount in excess of $ 19.5 million in tax rebate for promising not to move some business out of state. In actuality it showed up later that this amount was almost twice that initially estimated. In addition to this case of extortion there is also the latest in a tax-avoidance tactic known as "Inversion", where U.S. based companies will move their corporate head-quarters to a country with lower corporate taxes. They in effect stop being a U.S. company for tax purposes. As a case in point pharmaceutical giant Pfizer announced a merger with Allergan, a firm located in Dublin, where the new headquarters would be situated. By applying a practice called "earnings strip-ping" they will be able to lower their taxable U.S. profits. Using this strategy, the U.S. subsidiary of the inverted company (formerly the headquarters) can take a loan from its foreign parent company. The interest payments of that debt can then be deducted from the U.S. company's taxable income and is taxable at the lower rate in the new "parent" company's country of registra-tion. In the case of Pfizer it has been rumored that this maneuver would reduce their US tax bill from 25.5 to 17 %, or about $ 35 billion.

These two cases are by no means alone or unique.

In both of those cases nothing material has altered. The companies are still relying on state and local services and the financing of infrastructure like roads, schools, bridges and maintenance of all the utilities. And their employees still send the children to local schools. This all costs money. This money comes primarily from the taxes paid, personal, business and property taxes.

Therefore, when the large multinational companies take steps to avoid paying their due taxes, by applying write-offs and by shuffling of monies between overseas holding companies, the resulting tax burden falls on smaller businesses and ordinary wage earners. Most of these tax evaders are hugely profitable and could easily afford to pay their normal taxes, however in their never ceasing strive to satisfy Wall Street's expectations, they don't. And it is legal. But it is grossly unethical and damaging to the American economy. And on study found that these tax dodging practices by major corporations cost the U.S. Treasury over $ 100 billion a year. That amount of money could indeed make a big difference in a lot of important government programs. It might even mean that a lot of programs will have to be cut back.

An equally debilitating effect of this tax avoidance phenomenon is the damage it does to the fabric of the democratic society. When payroll taxes have to make up for the reductions in corporate taxes two things happen; first the full tax burden is shifted to the lower earners in society and secondly the feeling of unfairness for those individuals is vastly increased. There is a breech of society's contract which states that everyone pays according to ability. When the corporate world enjoys all the goods and services while leaving it to the rest of society to foot the bill it leaves a feeling of having been cheated. Some of the members are not paying their dues!

This corrosion of trust and solidarity was further exacerbated with the recent revelation of the Panama Papers held by Panamanian law firm and corporate service provider Mossack Fonseca. The leaked documents illustrate how wealthy individuals, including public officials, are able to keep personal financial information private. While the use of offshore business entities is often not illegal, reporters found that some of the shell corporations were used for illegal purposes, including fraud, kleptocracy, tax evasion, and evading international sanctions.

These tax dodging activities, while legal raise an important question of morality. The current system has created an atmosphere where the incentives to use all and every tax loop hole far outweigh the ethical question of shared responsibility. And of course the large corporate entities can apply unlimited resources in the endeavor to reduce their tax exposure.

So, this corporate practice of avoiding paying tax at any cost comes at a great cost to society at large.

The duty to pay society's annual "Membership Fees" has been eloquently expressed by Elizabeth Warren, the U.S. Senator from Massachusetts with the following statement:

"There is nobody in this country, who got rich on his own. Nobody. You built a factory out there – good for you. But I want to be clear. You moved your goods to market on the roads the rest of us paid for. You hired workers the rest of us paid to educate. You were safe in your factory because of police forces and fire forces that the rest of us paid for. You didn't have to worry that marauding bands would come and seize everything at your factory...

Now look. You built a factory and it turned into something terrific or a great idea – God bless! Keep a big hunk of it. But part of the under-lying social contract is you take a hunk of that and pay forward for the next kid who comes along." [ELIZABETH WARREN]

During a campaign in 1936 Franklin Roosevelt said that:

"Here is my principle: Taxes shall be levied according to the ability to pay. That is the only American principle."

This expresses the social contract that everybody should honor. Everyone has enjoyed the available amenities and support of institutions and services on their way to making a living and supporting a family – services and infrastructure that all citizens have paid for. It is only Common Sense that you demonstrate your appreciation and solidarity by paying your fair share of that burden – to the best of your ability at any given point in your life.

(Common sense is-not so common!)

To BETTER ILLUSTRATE how the absence of common sense can create needless complications and confrontations, we have in the following chosen a few articles from daily newspapers, mainly the Seattle Times. The "Harpist" story is a clear example of the tyranny of the few over the many. This article also demonstrates how well meaning regulation can be misconstrued to harm and hinder rather than to help.

Although some of these articles appear dated, the topics mentioned and the common sense issues involved are timeless.

Seattle Times (02.16.07)

A dozen university students at Seattle University attempted a 96-hour "media deprivation" experiment. No listening to iPods or car radios. No checking e-mail. No chatting on cell phones. No surfing web sites such as MySpace.com or Facebook.com. No watching Desperate Housewives *or* The Daily Show *with John Stewart. It was eventually scaled back and in the end announced a failure.*

This is a terrible sign of the times, when silence becomes the enemy. It gives an indication that kids today are wired for sound and that they are feeling very uncomfortable, maybe even scared, if they are left alone with silence.

Along those same lines, it is now getting almost impossible to find a quiet spot in the nation's airports. In every seating area, television sets emit a constant barrage of news stories, talk shows, and sports events. This forced-noise environment can almost be labeled "cruel and unjust treatment." It certainly does not provide calm and serenity, which is so needed in today's business of air travel.

As we get to live closer and closer to one another, the need for "Quiet Zones" will become more indispensable. More attention will be paid to sound emitters such as movable machine warning noises, lawn mowers, leaf blowers and of course radios and other electronic media. The latter can of course be regulated by hand, whereas the former involves advances by science and engineering efforts. It requires that people show a lot more consideration and awareness of how they and their noise sources may disturb the peace of others.

Seattle Times (02.16.07)

Immigrant advocates and two local religious leaders said Thursday that they would launch a program to offer sanctuary to illegal immigrants if the federal government continues to raid work sites and deport individuals without fixing its immigration system.

There is currently a law on the books that makes illegal immigration illegal! So, aiding and abetting these people and thus flouting the law in the name of human compassion is just wrong-and also illegal.

Seattle Times (02.15.07)

A shopping mall where five people were gunned down this week reopened Wednesday as authorities tried to figure out why a Bosnian immigrant committed the rampage and how he got his hands on a pistol. "We are going to look at where he got the gun," said Lori Dyer, in charge of the local ATF office.

Well, why is it such a mystery to the authorities that this man—or any other perpetrator, for that matter—could easily get a handgun? In a society where limiting access to handguns is akin to sacrilege, there are automatically going to be a lot of handguns available.

"Elementary, my dear Watson!" or, "Common sense, my dear Watson."

One of the great mysteries in the debate on gun control is the fact that permits and vetting procedures apply to people buying guns from gun shops, but not to those buying their guns at gun shows. We are anxiously waiting for someone to explain that one. Maybe we should also let used car dealers sell driver's licenses together with the purchase of a car!

Seattle Times (08.21.07)
Sentinel Accused of Lying to Clients

Sentinel Management, the cash-management firm that froze client with-drawals last week, was sued by the Securities and Exchange Commission (SEC) for allegedly lying to investors and misappropriating their assets.

Sentinel fraudulently moved at least $460 million in securities from clients' accounts into its own accounts and misused customers' holdings as collateral to ob-tain a $321-million line of credit "for its own benefit," the SEC said in a lawsuit filed at U.S. District Court in Chicago. Sentinel's conduct put clients "at risk of serious and irreparable loss," the SEC said in its complaint.

The time has come when we start treating these horrendous, fraudulent practices as serious crimes. One has only to imagine the utter devastation to hundreds, if not thousands, of households to conclude that this is akin to murder. The perpetrators of such crimes should not be able to get away with spending only a couple of years in a "country club."

Seattle Times (February 2007)

2 Officers Charged in Teen's Death

A French judge has charged two police officers in connection with the electrocution of two teenagers. The two youths were electrocuted when they climbed into a power substation while trying to hide from police who were chasing them. A third youth who was injured said the teenagers, who were of African descent, had done nothing wrong but were afraid of being harassed by the police.

Ooh, la, la! How sad-that the law enforcement officers can be faulted for chasing suspected wrongdoers. If there is someone here who was doing something wrong, it surely must have been the judge.

Seattle Times (09.04.07): The Tyranny of the Few—Who Is More Secure?

Harpist isn't playing on ferry anymore

David Michael's Celtic harp has been silenced after more than 17 years of soothing ferry passengers traveling between Port Townsend and Keystone on Whidbey Island.

Washington State Ferries officials had received two complaints from passengers saying that they had to abide by security measures while Michael did not.

State ferries officials say they had no choice but to fairly enforce security policies that were stepped up after the Sept. 11 terrorist attacks.

Tightening security requires passengers to take their baggage and personal items off the ferries, even if they are returning on the next ferry run. They must also remain with their personal items, such as backpacks and luggage.

What that meant for Michael was lugging the 30-pound harp and packing CD's on and off each of eight departures and arrivals at the terminals.

So, now there is no more music on board the ferry because of the tyranny of a few complaining passengers, who apparently were not satisfied with the explanation that Michael did not pose a threat to the security of the ferry system. This was, of course, compounded by the inability of state officials to make an exception to the rules for fear of legal reprisals.

As Michael himself said, after his unsuccessful bid to have the decision overturned, "Nobody is checking out passengers more than me. So if there was something or somebody suspicious, I'm most likely the one who would turn them in."

Why didn't the state officials grant a special waiver for Michael by giving him a security clearance in the interest of satisfying the wishes of all of the other passengers? As for the two complainers, do they really think that the state ferry system is one iota safer after Michael stopped playing his harp?

Sunday Seattle Times (06.18.06)

On the front page of today's *Sunday Seattle Times,* there was an article with the heading, "Ex-security officials rake it in," and the brief summary:

*Dozens are collecting fat salaries as consultants or lobbyists for contractors doing business with divisions of their former federal departments. **And because of ethics loopholes, it's all legal.***

The problem is that last sentence. Ethics is a value system, not a legal system. The behavior is unethical; hence, it should not be done, especially not by well-educated pillars of society.

Atlanta (March 2005)

The defendant was scheduled to be arraigned in court on charges of having raped his girlfriend. The previous day he had tried to smuggle a knife into court manufactured from a doorknob, and that understandably made the court employees nervous.

In spite of this, and contrary to all wisdom and common sense, the defendant, on the day after this incident, was escorted from the holding cell to the courtroom by a female deputy, and without any shackles or cuffs of any kind. After he had changed into normal clothes from his prison garb, he easily managed to overpower the deputy, take her gun, and proceed to the courtroom, where he shot the presiding judge and the court stenographer. After causing this carnage in the courtroom, he escaped and commandeered (hijacked) a car, pistol-whipping the car's owner, and disappeared into Atlanta.

Why, was he not shackled and cuffed?

Well, a legal precedent had been established earlier whereby a defendant could not be brought into the courtroom appearing as a convict or as a guilty person, lest the jury be unduly influenced against him or her. Therefore, he had a change of clothes and was not restrained by handcuffs.

Well, why not use common sense? Here was a defendant who the previous day had shown that he was contemplating violence, and yet his civil liberties could not be violated.

That is not common sense!

To add further to this story, the whole police department of Atlanta, assisted by federal officers, could not find the murderer.

A young and very brave woman, Ashley Smith, endured the ordeal of being held as a hostage by this man, and managed to calm him enough to start reasoning with him. She made him see the evil of his ways and convinced him to face his punishment as one of God's children. She then left the apartment and called to tell the police that they could come and pick him up at her place.

The police arrived armed to the teeth in enough force to occupy a small country. Much to their apparent disappointment, he waved a white flag and let them arrest him without any resistance.

Following this successful end to the story, the chief of police held a press conference, where he praised his department and all of his officers for the tremendous effort and vigilance they had exhibited in the pursuit of this dangerous man.

Hello!! Is anybody home? They had been unable to find the perpetrator to these heinous crimes, and when a young mother delivered him to them on a silver platter, the chief of police bestowed praise on the officers of the law, who had been largely ineffective in their duties. "Ridiculous" is the word that comes to mind.

Star Ledger (03.19.05)

Gay owner of club denied funeral rites

Where is the forgiveness and the compassion of the Church when it refuses to honor a dead man's wishes for religious services just because he was running an adult entertainment business (or for being gay)?

Here is the "Christian" verdict:

"His business is adult entertainment, which is inconsistent with Catholic teaching."

"People would be scandalized that the church granted a funeral to a person who had this type of business activity."

If this is the teaching of a religion, then one should be happy to be an atheist. At least most atheists believe in being tolerant and compassionate.

Seattle Times (06.16.10)

Washington-The Office of Congressional Ethics (OCE) is investigating eight law-makers who held fundraisers within 48 hours of a major House vote on a Wall Street bill or received substantial donations from business people with a financial stake in the bill, according to congressional sources and letters.

Common sense tells you that these senators have set their GPS destination for the wrong address. Instead of working for their constituents, they are allegedly working for special interests (and themselves). See also **Chapter 4: Politicians-Serving Whom?**

Seattle Times (06.16.10)

On the video the police officer is seen punching the girl in the face after she tries to intervene in the arrest of a 19-year-old friend near Franklin High School on Monday afternoon. Police arrested the girl and her friend, both of whom have criminal records.

It should be said that the girl also pushed the officer before he struck her. So, the police officer was framed by the video, but the rest of the situation as it escalated was conveniently not documented. The verbal harassment by the friend and the resistance and pushing preceding the punch were not shown. Therefore, the incident should be seen as part of escalating and threatening behavior by the two girls.

With the breakdown of respect for the law in general and police officers in particular, even small incidents can quickly escalate. Every attempt by police to solve a dispute is automatically met with resistance and verbal abuse. So whose fault is it that the situation gets out of hand in spite of the officer's attempt to control the situation?

Being a police officer in America today is indeed a thankless job. He is damned if he does and damned if he doesn't. The police are tasked to uphold the law and to protect citizens from harm; if, in doing so, he happens to use force when restraining an unruly culprit, he will surely run the risk of being accused of brutality by the press and of being sued by the "innocent" wrongdoer.

Common sense tells us that we should all support the police force, which acts as a "firewall" between ordinary, law-abiding citizens and mayhem in the form of violence, disturbance, and destruction of property. Why is it, then, that the media seems to be defending the perpetrator and not the victim? To condone violence is to perpetrate violence.

(It must be said that the girls later apologized for their behavior.)

Not only crime alone, but fear of crime, can paralyze a community.

In America...

WHEN COVERING SUCH a varied topic as common sense one comes across a myriad of smaller anecdotal examples, which by themselves do not warrant extensive analysis and debate. These are just small fragments of information, and sentences which have the common characteristics that they appear to have elements of foolishness and contradiction – in other words, lack of common sense. Although the examples are taken from America, it is not to say that some cannot apply elsewhere in the world. Lack of common sense knows no borders.

In America, it is possible to legally grow and distribute the drug marijuana for medical and recreational use in one state, California, while at the same time this is illegal and a criminal offense under federal law. Maybe they just do not inhale in California!!

In America, it is possible to see large groups of illegal aliens congregate at shopping malls to sell their services, without apparently running the risk of being rounded up and deported. It appears that the users of these services, be it construction or yard work, have been able to shield these illegal workers from the arm of the law. Illegal in plain sight!

In America, the airlines make the default seat spacing so small that they can charge extra for the amount of leg room, which should have been the standard from the beginning.

In America, they have areas around schools designated as "no weapon" and "no drug" zones. Is the implicit message that it's okay to carry weapons and sell/use drugs outside of these zones?

In America, cars are being marketed by TV ads that show how fast and by how much the legal speed limit can be exceeded.

In America, TV has hijacked public spaces. In doctors' and dentists' waiting rooms, in gyms, airports, hairdressers, and wherever else there is a captive audience, the TV is robbing you of peace and quiet, of a moment to reflect, read a book, or just sit back and think of nothing. Soon the only quiet place in public will be at home!

In America, the taxpayers support millionaire farmers while government is neglecting to update the essential infrastructure.

In America, why is the fight against organized crime so badly organized?

In America, more money is being spent on studying a problem than on actually solving it.

In America, adults preach the dangers of beer and wine to teenagers from the safe harbor of a well-stocked liquor cabinet.

In America, we can render quick and efficient assistance to tsunami victims in Indonesia and Thailand, thousands of miles from the homeland, but we are unable to put together an expedient and coherent effort to help victims of Katrina on the Gulf Coast shores.

In America, you can complain about the enormous problems of teenage pregnancies and at the same time be vehemently opposed to prevention and sex education.

In America, the rights of all are often seconded to the rights of one.

In America, you have a distribution of food, which in some parts results in a large segment of the population suffering from starvation and malnutrition, and in other parts results in large segments of the population spending huge amounts of money and energy in an attempt to shed the extra weight from overeating.

If the money and energy that at any given time is spent in the name of weight loss could be used to feed the hungry, there might not be any left—hungry, that is!

In America, famous sports stars refuse to submit to drug testing on the grounds that they have nothing to hide.

In America, people hide their uniqueness under a cover of conformity.

In America, the complexities of life are reduced to mere sound bites.

In America, you can send your dog to a spa with all the conveniences, including psychoanalysis and pedicure, while children huddle in the backseats of abandoned cars, cold, hungry, and forgotten.

In America, you lose your health care plan when you lose your job.

In America, your tax burden is inversely proportional to your wealth.

In America, there is so much freedom of religion that an individual religion can no longer freely conduct its customary celebrations for fear of offending other religions. So instead of America having a multitude of different religious faiths lending their own special color to the annual celebrations and events, religious celebrations and expressions are no longer being tolerated, courtesy of the ever-vigilant zealots and lawyers.

When the "Land of the Free" has reached the point where you can no longer say the word "Christmas," we are slowly reaching a state of religious oppression akin to the situation in former communist Russia.

In America, there is separation of Church and State guaranteed by the Constitution. It is very hard to discern this separation since so much points in a different direction.

In America, it is quite common for public figures, movie stars, sports icons, and politicians, when they have done or said something that was deemed offensive by any one of the media groups, to later apologize with the explanation, "That's not what I meant", "If that's what was said, I did not mean it," or "I am deeply sorry." After this public cleansing ceremony, they can go on as if nothing happened. And they can again adopt the opinions and behavior for which they were publicly lambasted and humiliated, albeit this time they keep quiet.

In America, the same people who walk around blowing leaves with a noisy, energy-consuming air blower are the ones complaining that their jobs do not leave them with enough time to go to the fitness center.

In America, there is plenty-for the few!!

In America, the prison population is swelling to such proportions that it is soon going to be difficult to see who is actually on the outside and who is on the inside.

In America, we seem to be much more compassionate toward the Indians of Peru and Brazil than we are towards the Indians of Colorado and Arizona.

In America, the government sponsors foreign language education to new immigrants in an attempt to better assimilate them into the English-speaking community.

In America, in another twenty years, education is going to become so expensive that no one can afford to buy one.

In America, if an event happens outside the U.S. and no U.S. citizens are involved then it's as if the event did not happen. In the same spirit of national euphoria, if a sports event is broadcast from somewhere in the world and if one American is participating, the whole broadcast will be concentrated on this one American, even if he finishes last.

In America, you need a license to drive a car, you need a permit to conduct business, and you need a certificate to build a house. If only a qualification were required to father a child!

In America, why do people wonder why so many have developed a destructive streak when everything happening between commercials on TV is aimed at glorifying the art of violence, mayhem, and destruction?

In America, freedom is cherished. You are free to buy a gun. You are free to buy ammunition. You are free to own a loaded gun. Driving while intoxicated is like playing with a loaded gun, but you are not free to drive while intoxicated.

In America, you can be caught for driving while intoxicated (DWI) many times; you will be fined many times, maybe even jailed for a short stint, but nobody seems to be able to stop your reckless behavior until they can get you for vehicular manslaughter. By then it is, of course, too late for the victim.

In America, the measures for product safety aimed at protecting children have been executed so successfully that many older adults have problems opening the packages in question. The seniors have as much chance as the children of getting access to the food and medicine because they lack the adequate strength. This is a typical example where lack of common sense has resulted in the creation of one serious problem when trying to solve another.

In America, you have to make a law forbidding drivers from texting while driving cars, as if that were not common sense. Maybe bicycles will be next!

In America, you have to pay your bills within thirty days, lest you run the risk of making irreparable damages to your credit rating. But when you are due a refund, the wait can be up to half a year.

In America, it is interesting to note how a vice chances to a virtue when, instead of serving the individual, it serves the community. Take gambling, for instance. When it serves the individual, it is deemed destructive both morally and financially. When it serves the community, it is revenue-enhancing and therefore a virtue. Only the thoughtless politician is willing to destroy the individual in the name of funding the community.

In America, or, more precisely, Hollywood, it is baffling to note that, with all the preparations and expensive props in the movies, why is it that you never see a full suitcase weighing anything? The actor is moving out of his home or is going on an extended holiday and has packed two large suitcases. It is clear, though, that when he runs down the street with these suitcases or when he throws them in the trunk of the car, there is nothing in them. Couldn't the director at least weigh down the suitcases with some bricks? Or would he have to pay the actors an additional bonus for doing the heavy lifting?

In America, the spirit of litigation fueled by the abundance of willing legal talent is threatening to destroy the business of doing business. Only when the cost of not doing business becomes prohibitive will this change.

In America, the airports do not offer free baggage carts – unlike the airports in the rest of the world. It is considered an added revenue source, where it should have been a free service to the old and weary travelers.

In America, when politicians and large firms have to make major decisions, they hire outside consultants, for which they pay handsomely. This enables them to choose a solution from which they can distance themselves. The fact that they already have the adequate talent within the company does not seem to count.

In America, the red light at intersections telling pedestrians not to cross should be relabeled. Instead of it being a stop (do not cross) sign, it should be changed to a "Cross at your own risk"-sign. That way instead of people committing misdemeanors they will just demonstrate shear stupidity – or simply getting killed.

In America, we sometimes get our priorities mixed up. In Stockholm, Sweden 3 U.S.-born scientists were awarded the Nobel Prize in Physics for the study of exploding stars which revealed that the expansion of the universe is accelerating! –and each of them 3 took home $0.5 million.

Meanwhile a few days before, on the last Sunday of September, a relative unknown Golf-player won the FedEx-cup on the 3rd playoff hole and took home $10 million.

Claus Windelev

When debating the issue of common sense, always remember that:

- If it's too good to be true, it most likely is.
- If a promise is unrealistic, it remains only that-a promise.
- A lie seldom travels alone.
- If someone appears to be on a pedestal, it's probably because you are on your knees.
- If you travel as a group, the destination is not of your choice.
- The shortest distance between two points is a straight line.

Conclusion

THIS BOOK IS meant as a help for greater awareness of the need to think about what goes on around us and to try to use our intelligence and experience to arrive at common-sense solutions. This means solutions that make sense and serve the greater good of society.

In the beginning of this book we defined "Common sense" as being the "knack of seeing things as they are, and doing things as they ought to be done."

This sounds straight forward, were it not for the fact that each individual has a different perception of how things are and other ideas as to how things ought to be. There are different ways of looking at the world, even from the same vantage point and there are differences in experiences from one person to the next. So, one would conclude that something making sense to one individual would not necessarily make sense to another. This holds true in a lot of instances where personal habits and behavioral preferences are concerned and each individual has learned what makes good sense to them for a variety of life's challenges.

The word "common" indicates that we are talking about more than one person. As a matter of fact as you have been able to see from the content of this book we are talking about the whole nation of three hundred plus million living and thinking individuals. For so many people to be able to coexist in an amicable and productive manner, a certain common sense of perception and objective has to be present.

Through the depiction of a number of different topics the book is raising awareness of some areas and practices where the overall mission for an equal and just society has become subordinate to more narrow and personalized objectives. There is an increased stratification which could result in even further distance between the haves and the have-nots. This polarization of society is not only economic but also social.

One of the more serious developments threatening our democracy as pointed out in several of the chapters is the deterioration of public discourse. We are loosing the ability to converse when the words have no meaning and when we are confused by the different interpretations of the truths. Both have a debilitating effect on the healthy functioning of our democracy.

We need to act as an all-inclusive society with empathy and compassion towards the weaker citizens and support and encouragement towards the stronger productive citizens. This includes being true to our human values and accept that each and everyone of us should be responsible to the best of our ability. Everyone who has the ability also has the obligation.

When the majority sees the things as they are, they can also do things as they ought to be done. That is referred to as "COMMON SENSE".

Bibliography

Born in Denmark in 1943 during the German occupation, Claus Windelev developed an interest in world affairs at an early age. His love for exploring the diversity of human cultures led him to extensive travels around the globe. He always kept an open mind and tried to understand the differences between peoples. An engineer by profession, Mr. Windelev is fluent in several languages, as well as being a celebrated painter. Mr. Windelev is also the author of the books, "Ethics – for you and the rest of the world" and "Common Sense – an Outsider's look from the Inside".

www.ingramcontent.com/pod-product-compliance
Lightning Source LLC
Chambersburg PA
CBHW071348280526
45787CB00001B/257